What Others Are Saying About
8 Steps to Achieve Your Destiny...

Samuel Chand is a leader's leader. His keen insights and vast leadership exposure have prepared him well for resourcing the kingdom. His natural passion for leadership development is a refined gift he enthusiastically shares with leaders and developing leaders.

—Dr. John C. Maxwell
The John Maxwell Company and EQUIP

"This magnificent book by my friend Dr. Sam Chand will give you a practical understanding of pain, pressure, and your potential. Read this book to have your perspective forever transformed."

—John Bevere
Author, founder of Messenger International

"Sam Chand's insights will help any leader successfully face the inevitable challenges that all leaders must face. Sam is a brilliant communicator and this book is a must-read for anyone who wants to become a stronger, wiser, more compassionate leader."

—Jentezen Franklin
Senior Pastor, Free Chapel
Author of New York Times bestseller, Fasting

"Given the many leaders who are imploding right before our eyes, this is a timely discussion from a capable resource! I pray you'll give Dr. Chand's thoughts deep contemplation, whether you are a leader or you serve one!"

—*Bishop T. D. Jakes Sr.*
Best-selling author
Pastor, The Potter's House of Dallas

"Dr. Chand has been one of the most valuable mentors in my life and ministry. He has tremendous character, valuable leadership insight, a contagious sense of humor, and a pastor's heart. He has mentored me and made me a much stronger spiritual leader."

—*Craig Groeschel*
Pastor, Lifechurch.tv
Edmond, Oklahoma

**STEPS TO ACHIEVE
YOUR DESTINY**

SAMUEL R. CHAND

STEPS TO ACHIEVE YOUR DESTINY

LEAD YOUR LIFE WITH PURPOSE

WHITAKER
HOUSE

8 STEPS TO ACHIEVE YOUR DESTINY:
Lead Your Life with Purpose
(Previously published as *LadderShifts*.)

ISBN: 978-1-62911-734-8
eBook ISBN: 978-1-62911-735-5
Printed in the United States of America
© 2006, 2016 by Dr. Samuel R. Chand

Samuel R. Chand Consulting, Inc.
950 Eagles Landing Parkway, Suite 295
Stockbridge, GA 30281 USA
www.samchand.com

Whitaker House
1030 Hunt Valley Circle
New Kensington, PA 15068
www.whitakerhouse.com

Library of Congress Cataloging-in-Publication Data
LC record available at https://lccn.loc.gov/2016029480

1 2 3 4 5 6 7 8 9 10 11 **W** 23 22 21 20 19 18 17 16

ACKNOWLEDGMENTS

You never "achieve your destiny" by yourself. My wife, Brenda, has helped me at each step. Thank you for being my best ladder-holder. Thanks for believing in me.

CONTENTS

INTRODUCTION: STRATEGIC SHIFTS

As I've worked with leaders of businesses, churches, and non-profits, I've been privileged to watch remarkable leaders who have instituted bold changes and seen remarkable growth. However, I've also observed a few leaders who seemed completely satisfied with the status quo. No matter how much we talked about reaching higher goals and changing more lives, they found excuses to remain stuck in old patterns of thinking, perceiving, and leading. To make progress, leaders have to make strategic shifts in their attitudes and behavior.

TWO CHALLENGES

All leaders face two different challenges: *responding* to change around them and *initiating* change in their organizations. Both of these challenges are shifting circumstances for a leader, and both require the leader to take steps in order to be more effective.

TWO ERRORS

Leaders are prone to two types of errors: *failing to take the necessary steps* and *taking steps without wisdom and patience*. Some leaders become paralyzed by the threat of change. They may realize change is necessary, but the risk of failure or criticism renders them immobile. Other leaders have the opposite response: they act impulsively—without adequate planning, consultation with others, or consideration of the consequences of their actions.

TWO KINDS OF PEOPLE

All organizations have two kinds of people: *the leader* who is providing vision, strategy, and hope, and *the people* who will implement those plans. Selecting the right implementers is essential!

TWO PERSPECTIVES

All leaders choose between two distinct perspectives: "*The old ways are good enough;* we just need to try harder" and "We need to take the blinders off, see new possibilities and new strategies, and *find the courage to take wise, bold steps forward.*" The way we view an opportunity or a challenge makes all the difference.

The old axiom says, "People instinctively resist change." That may be true for most people, but not for real leaders. Real leaders *create* change. They look for opportunities, find new ways to get things done, invest in new technologies, and initiate change, because they know that risk has the inherent potential of great reward.

But of course, risk also carries the possibility of failure. I'm not advocating risk for the thrill of it. Instead, I'm recommending careful analysis, good planning, and acquiring the necessary resources so that risks offer the greatest hope of reward—for the leader and every person in the organization.

The kind of strategic steps I recommend in this book aren't reserved for the CEO of the most successful companies, the boards of Wall Street hedge funds, or the pastors of the largest churches in the country. These choices are necessary for all leaders—those in large and small organizations; those with degrees in leadership and those who have learned on the job; and those who have been leading for decades and those who are just starting out. If we keep our eyes open, we'll see possibilities where we only saw limitations in the past.

EIGHT STRATEGIC STEPS

In this book, we will look at eight different but very common choices. The progress of our organizations depends on how we respond to these challenges.

1. New People

The people around us have helped us come this far, and we are deeply grateful for their contribution and love. We may discover, however, that the ones who helped us climb to two hundred in attendance or a million in sales aren't the same people who can take us to five hundred or ten million. They are wonderful people, but at least some of them may have limited capacity for growth and a limited vision for the future.

To climb higher, we need to find a higher caliber of men and women who are stronger in basic leadership skills, better communicators, and outstanding visionaries who see more possibilities. As we identify new people and replace those who have served faithfully, our task is to make this shift with grace, honoring those who have faithfully served and finding a place where they can continue to devote their energies and their hearts. Then, with new people around us, we will be able to climb higher—until we reach the limit of their skills and vision, and we find new people again.

2. New Pains

Leadership always creates pain, because necessary change makes many people feel uncomfortable. As I wrote in *Leadership Pain*, "You'll grow only to the threshold of your pain." If your goal is to avoid pain, you'll avoid challenges, but you'll also miss out on growth and opportunities for success. If you want to stretch yourself, your leadership team, and your organization toward greatness, you'll necessarily encounter plenty of painful choices and reactions. Get used to it. Welcome it, because it's your best teacher. And become a willing and eager student of pain's lessons.

3. New Places

We often talk about "where our organization needs to go." The destination—defined by our vision, mission, and goals—is a "place" where we want to go, just like Yellowstone National Park is a place we may want to go on vacation. To get to our organization's desired future, we need to evaluate our vehicle: our strategies, staff, and structures. We keep what will take us farther and we replace the worn or unused parts that slow us down. When we chart a new path to an unknown area of business or ministry, we can expect some thrills, some surprises, and some setbacks. That's the nature of adventures! To get where we want to go, we need plenty of courage, which is our fuel for the journey.

4. New Perspectives

Leaders are learners. We stop growing (and we stop being effective leaders) when we stop searching for new ways to see reality around us. The best leaders are humble enough to know what they don't know, and they find people to fill the void in their thinking. They read, they listen, and they find a mentor who can help them take the next step. When they initiate change, these leaders discover that the going gets rough, the people around them can no longer keep up, and the temptation to go back to when things were easier may seem enticing. New perspectives inevitably produce a fair share of difficulties. Failure and chaos are part of life when we try new ways of thinking about life and leadership. The best leaders get excited about learning and innovation, and they welcome a good push to help them move forward.

5. New Priorities

Leaders realize that everything isn't of equal importance, but those who are in the middle of instituting change realize they have to be ruthless to restructure their priorities. Old ways may have worked very well for a simpler and more limited vision, but reaching greater heights requires a new plan that will demand an investment of time, people, and other resources. Good leaders realize they don't only need a new vision of the future, they also need to define the steps to reach their new goals, including a system to monitor their organization's progress. New priorities, then, must be both inspiring and practical.

6. New Passions

In different seasons of their careers, leaders can become exhausted from overwork, or perhaps bored from work that has become too familiar and comfortable. Also, the seasons of life change as we age, and we may need to initiate changes in order to find new sources of strength and joy. Don't let the familiar become a tomb! If life has become exhausting or boring, make a change. Discover (or rediscover) energy and excitement in your most important relationships and in your work. Take a vacation (and turn your cell phone off most of every day), take up a new hobby, write a book, or get a degree in a field that interests you. Whatever it takes, be a person with a zest for life!

7. New preparations

When we make strategic shifts so we can reach new places and reach higher than ever before, our old daily habits will no longer be adequate. We need to take stock in how we prepare our bodies, our minds, and our hearts; how we sharpen our skills; and how we equip and motivate the key people around us. Some leaders are so gifted they get by without any preparation, but that only works to a certain point. To reach higher and do more, we all need to acquire new skills and develop better habits of preparation.

8. New Possibilities

Insecure leaders feel threatened by challenges. They react defensively, trying to control people and situations to avoid failure. Secure, humble, wise leaders are realistic about the problems they face, but they remain full of hope. They develop a genuine joy as they face new possibilities. In fact, they have an essential quality of great leadership: "change readiness," the willingness to enthusiastically embrace risks and opportunities. Instead of withdrawing from challenges, they find creative ways to respond, always taking people with them on the journey. And these leaders realize the incredible resource of modern technology to communicate with this generation.

LOOKING FORWARD

My friend, you've been accomplishing a lot, but do you realize that you can do so much more? I know you are eager to make those strategic shifts and reach those greater heights. How do I know? Because you're reading this book!

As I've consulted with pastors and business leaders, I've seen them make changes that have propelled them to new levels of effectiveness. They've paid a price, but they would all say, "It's been well worth it!"

As a leader, your biggest challenge isn't money, staff members, building plans, or marketing strategies. The most important challenge you face isn't "out there," it's "in here"—in your perceptions and attitudes. As you read these eight chapters and gain insights about the roadblocks you can overcome, you'll find new ways to respond to the situations and people around you. You'll implement strategic shifts and you'll become more effective. That's what leadership is all about—making sense of what's happening in your environment and making changes to move your organization forward. As you learn and grow, you'll be able to help others learn and grow, too. You'll climb higher toward your destiny and you'll prepare the leaders around you to face the challenges in their journeys.

Don't settle for the status quo. Respond with wisdom and courage to the shifts in our culture, and initiate plenty of your own shifts to create an atmosphere of creativity, hope, and excitement in your organization.

1

NEW PEOPLE

"My main job was developing talent. I was a gardener providing water and other nourishment to our top 750 people. Of course, I had to pull out some weeds, too."[1]
—Jack Welch

Paul was sweating. His largest client had just called, asking for earlier completion of an important project. Paul had been up nearly all night, scrambling for ways to meet his regular project deadlines. Despite the success of his small software company, he found it increasingly difficult to retain responsible employees. While there was no shortage of qualified programmers, their inability to meet deadlines or to even show up for work had forced him to let a number of them go. His most talented people were frequently lured away by offers from larger companies. Staring at the ringing phone, Paul wondered if he could afford to hire someone to deal with these human resource challenges.

---

1. Jack Welch quoted by Jeffrey E. Garten, "Jack Welch: A Role Model for Today's CEO?" *Bloomberg Business*, September 9, 2001, http://www.bloomberg.com/bw/stories/2001-09-09/jack-welch-a-role-model-for-todays-ceo.

Leadership is filled with "people issues." No leader is immune to them; they come with the territory. Like Paul, maybe you find yourself in need of some new people in your life. Perhaps you're wondering why you're not getting the support you need from people who have always been helpful in the past. Maybe you wish you could find someone to simply validate the challenges that you're dealing with, or provide sage advice from their own experience.

THE PEOPLE WHO GOT YOU TO WHERE YOU ARE NOW MAY NOT BE THE ONES WHO WILL TAKE YOU WHERE YOU NEED TO GO.

All leaders need new people in their lives. The people who got you to where you are now may not be the ones who will take you where you need to go. The chief financial officer (CFO) who took you from one million to five million may not be the one who takes you from five million to fifty million. As a leader, you have to accept the fact that your CFO has his own thresholds, his own limitations, and his own issues to work through. You have to accept that his perspective may be different than yours.

PEOPLE YOU WILL ENCOUNTER

There are many types of people leaders will work with and encounter. As you climb your career ladder, you'll encounter people who are where you were, where you are, and where you will/want to be.

In particular, there are eight different kinds of people, and many of the difficulties you'll encounter will come from not knowing how to deal with the issues and situations

WHEN YOU DON'T KNOW HOW TO ENGAGE AND DISENGAGE WITH PEOPLE, THERE WILL BE PAIN.

raised by these different groups of people. When you don't know how to engage and disengage with people, there will be pain. So let's take a closer look at these groups. Knowing about them can help you to deal with them appropriately. There are…

1. Positive and negative people

2. People you've outgrown

3. People who are tied to yesterday's solutions

4. "That's not my job" people

5. People who cannot move on

6. People who give you new perspective

7. People you can be transparent with

8. People who celebrate your success

Positive and Negative People

First, you'll encounter both positive and negative people. It's easy to recognize positive people; they are the ones who add value to your life. As you move up your ladder, it's important to have positive people around you. We all were created with a built-in need for approval, and we want to be around people who add value by agreeing or disagreeing with us. Understand that agreement is not always positive and disagreement is not always negative; people can disagree with us and still add value.

But there are some people who will not agree with us at all. What can you do about these people? What strategy can you use with them? I once heard a very insightful remark from the former president of Kenya. During our discussion, he said, "To appease everybody is to invite trouble."

When a company or an organization grows, you will find yourself appeasing fewer and fewer people. Appeasement involves finding the middle of the road, or compromising. The more you travel in the middle of the road, the more mediocrity you're going to produce. Excellence is found on the edges, never in the middle. Saying yes to one group or person and no to another invites challenges on both sides.

EXCELLENCE IS FOUND ON THE EDGES, NEVER IN THE MIDDLE.

Many times, when a negative person gives you his opinion, he will expect you to heed his advice. That's why it's important to be around people who are willing to give you input, whether in agreement or disagreement with you, without a demanding spirit. These are the positive people, the ones who will add value to your life and help you to get where you want to go.

People You've Outgrown

Second, you also must deal with people you've outgrown. Growing is necessary; it's what keeps you moving. There will be times when you outdistance the folks who started the journey with you. Maybe there's someone who was an integral part of your organization but who just hasn't grown with you. People have to understand that if they don't grow, they've got to go.

PEOPLE HAVE TO UNDERSTAND THAT IF THEY DON'T GROW, THEY'VE GOT TO GO.

The same thing can happen in a church. Perhaps you begin with twenty-five, thirty, or even one hundred people in your congregation. As you add many more people and expand to two or more services, you might find that the elders, board members, or other leaders who accompany you are not the same ones who will take you where you need to go. As a leader, you have to accept those facts.

People Who Are Tied to Yesterday's Solutions

People who are tied to yesterday's solutions are another concern. Dealing with the old guard is an issue that every leader has to wrestle with. In the early stages of an organization business, or church, leaders tend to throw people into positions. Perhaps when you began your church, you just wanted someone to play the keyboard. You weren't concerned about the person's musical pedigree. If he could read music and make a pretty sound, he was capable of leading worship. If you and your son started a landscaping business, for instance, you would not be too considered about hiring people with vast experience. You would just be looking for someone who was breathing and who could come to work and push a lawn mower. So maybe you would hire your son's friend, who is also your neighbor.

DEALING WITH THE OLD GUARD IS AN ISSUE THAT EVERY LEADER HAS TO WRESTLE WITH.

Then, after a certain amount of growth, leaders begin refining their approach and looking for expertise. This is when they realize that some people aren't working out. Maybe the people you've chosen don't understand what you want, don't want to learn contemporary worship songs, or wonder what's wrong with the way they've always done things. What do you do with them? Yesterday's solutions have become today's problems.

And because the young man you hired to push the lawn mower is your son's friend, your son may not like it when you let him go. Your neighbor may not like it, either. People will object. This is why issues that arise over yesterday's solutions are often complicated.

"That's Not My Job" People

Then there are the "that's not my job" people. When you hire people, they're typically tied to job descriptions. At higher levels, you are less concerned with job descriptions than you are with the presence of three essential characteristics: competency, character, and chemistry.

YESTERDAY'S SOLUTIONS HAVE BECOME TODAY'S PROBLEMS.

Competency is about the skills, the training, and the experience required to get the job done. Character is about integrity. What do people do when nobody is watching him or her? Leaders want people with integrity, whom they can trust. Last, there is chemistry, which, when missing, can really cause issues. It asks, "Does this person fit in?" "Can he or she get along with other people?" Carly Fiorina was the first outsider to lead Hewlett-Packard. When she left, many people attributed her departure to her chemistry with the company. She just didn't fit in with the culture of HP.

Southwest Airlines is a prime example of the great results you can achieve when employees have the right blend of competency, character, and chemistry. A man concerned about his elderly mother's ability to change flights in Tulsa called the Southwest Airlines ticket counter in Dallas, from where she would depart. The ticket agent personally volunteered to drive the woman to the airport, to fly with her from Dallas to Tulsa after his shift, and to ensure that she made the connection.

You want people like that—people who aren't restricted by the circumstances under which they were hired.

YOU WANT PEOPLE WHO TAKE OWNERSHIP OF A SITUATION INSTEAD OF SAYING, "THAT'S NOT MY JOB."

You want people who take ownership of a situation instead of saying, "That's not my job."

People Who Cannot Move On

You also have to cope with people who cannot move on. A leader is always dynamic, while organizations tend to be static. Sometimes, the vision and the movement of a leader do not mirror the vision and movement of the organization. We call that tension a lack of organizational congruence or alignment.

...YOU HAVE TO FIGURE OUT WHO IS GOING TO TAKE THE JOURNEY WITH YOU AND WHO IS NOT.

Carly Fiorina's vision of merging HP and Compaq caused a great deal of organizational tension. She had to battle employees, shareholders, and even board members. Her vision was out of sync with the organization.

When you have moved on and others have not, you have to figure out who is going to take the journey with you and who is not. You have to think about where you're going and who can help you get there.

People Who Give You New Perspective

It's also important that you find people who can give you new perspective. The most productive time of a new employee in any organization—secular or religious—is within the first three months. After that, they do not add the same value. In the first three months, they give you perspective by questioning the way you do things. They might say, "Didn't I just fill out a form that asked me for this same information?" New employees find redundancies and point out ineffectiveness. They find more effective ways of doing things, and they bring new ideas with them. After three months, they know that survival involves falling in step, so their DNA becomes that of the organization.

When I was president of a college, I always had conversations with new employees and their supervisors. I'd bring them together on the first day and encourage the new person to ask questions, and tell the supervisor not to be threatened

NEW PEOPLE BRING A UNIQUE PERSPECTIVE BECAUSE THEY SEE THINGS AT ANOTHER LEVEL.

by the questions. I'd tell them that those questions would help us to reconfigure and reinvent ourselves, and to make improvements. New people bring a unique perspective because they see things at another level. Oftentimes, you'll be able to recognize these change agents immediately by the fresh perspective they offer your organization/church/etc.

People You Can Be Transparent With

It's equally important to have people you can be transparent with. As you rise in leadership, it becomes increasingly difficult to find people you can talk to about your struggles. Since these are not issues you can talk about with just anybody, you need a few people in your life whom you can talk to, be transparent with, reveal your fears to, and count on to listen to your concerns. Chances are that the people you had conversations with two years ago may not be the same people you'll be having conversations with in years to come.

Why is it so difficult to find people to talk to? Because the stakes are higher. When your landscaping company consisted of just two men and a truck, you could talk about anything while driving down the road. But when you have ten trucks and one hundred employees, you're not going to talk to just anyone about the equipment you're going to buy, the plans you have to leverage your business, or whom you're going to let go.

There are fewer people who understand the reality of your position. You can find a lot of people to confide in when you're are at the two-men-and-a-truck level but fewer when the organization expands. It really can be lonely at the top—but it doesn't have to be.

People Who Celebrate Your Success

YOU WANT PEOPLE WHO WILL HELP YOU CELEBRATE YOUR JOURNEY.

You should also find people who celebrate your successes. The Scriptures tell us to weep with those who weep and rejoice with those who rejoice. (See Romans 12:15.) Unfortunately, people find it easier to weep with those who weep than to rejoice with those who rejoice.

Let's say that you and your friend start organizations at the same time; your organization takes off, but his is struggling. As a result, it may be very difficult for him to celebrate and rejoice with you.

You want people who will say, "Yeah, man! It's great that you're doing well!" You want people who can be the wind beneath your wings, who can cheer you along, who won't get jealous or envious, who won't disengage from you because you're doing well. You want people who will help you celebrate your journey.

PEOPLE PRINCIPLES

Every leader is tempted to ignore or dismiss one particular type of person. We dream about how much easier life would be without so-and-so, or how much better things would be if we could clone someone who is full of new ideas and is always encouraging.

But the fact is, we need different types of people in our lives. Rather than avoiding complicated people, leaders must focus on them. Jack Welch understood the importance of our dealings with people, and it helped him to transform stodgy General Electric into a highly competitive, multibillion-dollar global enterprise. Jack Welch, who has been called one of the greatest corporate leaders of this century, said he spent 50 percent of his time on people issues. That's taking your people seriously!

Businessweek reported that Welch told his senior managers that they should be proud of everyone that reported to them. If they weren't proud of their people, they weren't setting themselves up to win. And Welch established the example for his leaders to follow. He sent handwritten notes to production workers. He apologized to one executive's wife for keeping him tied up with an important presentation. He commended one of his executives who turned down a promotion that would have required his teenage daughter to transfer schools. In many companies, turning down a promotion is what's called a "career-limiting" move. But Jack Welch called this manager up and praised him for keeping his priorities straight.[2]

...THE WAY AN ORGANIZATION GROWS IS BY GROWING ITS PEOPLE. Jack Welch knew that the way an organization grows is by growing its people. Too many leaders think that the best way to expand a company is to develop a leading-edge product or a service that blows all competition away. We try to convince ourselves that the best way to grow a congregation is to have appealing programs, inspiring services, and a magnificent building. But that's not going to produce long-term growth. To grow your church or organization, grow your leaders in number and in depth.

Achieving growth comes from keeping these three "people principles":

+ People Principle #1: To grow your organization, grow your people. To grow as a leader, grow other leaders.

---

2. John A. Byrne, "How Jack Welch Runs GE: A Close-up Look at How America's #1 Manager Runs GE," *BusinessWeek*, June 8, 1998.

+ People Principle #2: Surround yourself with people who challenge you to grow.

+ People Principle #3: Focus on your organization's context, not its packaging.

People Principle #1: To grow your organization, grow your people. To grow as a leader, grow other leaders.

"Growing" people is a very holistic process. It involves helping them develop competency, character, and chemistry.

To help them developing competency, send them to classes, seminars, and workshops that help them to develop their skill, so they become a better widget maker, computer person, or musician. Whatever their talent, make sure they cultivate it!

To develop character, pay attention to people's decisions and make sure they are ethical. Ensure that they err on the side of losing business rather than engaging in shady business.

TO GROW YOUR CHURCH OR ORGANIZATION, GROW YOUR LEADERS IN NUMBER AND IN DEPTH.

To develop chemistry, help them to strengthen people skills, leadership skills, and management skills. Typically, people don't leave organizations because of competency issues. They leave because they don't fit in with the culture, because they either don't know how or don't want to develop chemistry with the organization. Most people I've had to let go fall into this category.

Growing people must be a holistic effort. Many companies have on-site fitness facilities and wellness benefits, but imagine if your organization sponsored a marriage retreat for employees. If an employee's marriage is strong, won't he be more productive? If an employee isn't distracted by a divorce, won't she give the job her full attention? Isn't it better if your employee doesn't have to work a second job to make ends meet? Growing people means caring for the many facets of their well-being. After all, you want the whole person coming to work every day.

People Principle #2: Surround yourself with people who challenge you to grow.

Everyone is familiar with the undesirable yes-man. Concerned only with protecting his status and position, he never disagrees with his leaders. Have you ever considered what your life would be like if you were surrounded by yes-men?

If we surround ourselves with people who are just like us, our weaknesses will never be challenged. We must complement our weaknesses within the organization. John Maxwell says, "Staff your weaknesses." Find out where you're weak, and hire people with strengths in those areas. Most pastors are not good with finances. We went to school to study theology, not financial management. As a result, we don't know how to read an audit or answer an accountant's questions. If that's you, stop pretending and hire someone with that competency!

When you need to hire, look for someone who is better than you. If you want to stay where you are and make lateral moves, hire people just like you. People who are just like you will never challenge you to grow. When Scripture talks about iron sharpening iron (see Proverbs 27:17), it's talking about people who will sharpen, or challenge, your thinking. You should surround yourself with people who think up new ideas and challenge the status quo. And give them permission to speak honestly, so that you grow. You don't have to agree about everything. You might walk away saying, "Well, we didn't agree, but it sure gave me something to think about."

You have to be secure enough to let someone else fill in where you are weak. Don't pretend that you have to do everything yourself. Insecure people will hire people who lack competency, character, and chemistry. Secure leaders will hire people who excel in these attributes, who may be even better than they are. I can walk into any church or organization and determine how secure the leader is by observing the people. If the leader has gathered eagles around him, I know he's an eagle. If he's gathered turkeys around him, I don't care how much he says he's an eagle, he's just a turkey.

It is better to be alone than in the wrong company.

Tell me who your best friends are, and I will tell you who you are. If you run with wolves, you will learn how to howl. But if you associate with eagles, you will learn how to soar to great heights. *"A mirror reflects a man's face, but what he is really like is shown by the kind of friends he chooses"* (Proverbs 27:19 TLB). The simple but true fact of life is that you become like those whom you closely associate with—for the good and the bad.

The less you associate with some people, the more your life will improve. When you tolerate mediocrity in others, you will become mediocre. An important attribute in successful people is their impatience with negative thinking and negative-acting people. As you grow, your associates will change. Some of your friends will not want you to move on; they will want you to stay where they are. Friends who don't help you climb will make you crawl. Your friends will either stretch your vision or choke your dream. Those who don't increase you will eventually decrease you.

Here are some helpful tips to avoid these pitfalls:

+ Never receive counsel from unproductive people.

+ Never discuss your problems with a person incapable of contributing to the solution. Not everyone has a right to speak into your life. You are certain to get the worst of the bargain when you exchange ideas with the wrong person. Often, unsuccessful people are always first to tell you how to do things.

+ Don't follow anyone who's not going anywhere. With some people you spend an evening; with others you invest it.

+ Be careful where you stop to inquire for directions along the road of life.

> "Wise is the person who fortifies his life
> with the right friendships."
> —Anonymous

People Principle #3: Focus on your organization's context, not its packaging.

Writer and business expert Tom Peters says that your company will never experience a talent shortage as long as it's a great place to work. A growing organization attracts qualified people, so it doesn't have to hire people with cold resumes. Growing organizations and churches are filled with people who want to be a part of them.

It's not the stock options, fringe benefits, or salary that attract people. It's not the product or service, either. What attracts people is becoming part of an organization that's going somewhere, that's doing something, that's changing the world.

Apple cofounder Steve Jobs tried to convince John Sculley to leave his job as senior vice president of PepsiCo to become the CEO of Apple. Sculley wasn't particularly interested in leaving a secure position at Pepsi to help run this brand-new company. Jobs changed that by asking him, "Do you want to spend the rest of your life selling sugared water or do you want a chance to change the world?" Being part of a company that was doing something important is what attracted John Sculley to Apple.

> **WHAT ATTRACTS PEOPLE IS BECOMING PART OF AN ORGANIZATION THAT'S GOING SOMEWHERE, THAT'S DOING SOMETHING, THAT'S CHANGING THE WORLD.**

Herb Kelleher, cofounder and former chairman of Southwest Airlines, said that the company probably has twenty-five applicants for every open job.[3] That's not because the company has been consistently profitable; it's because people want to be connected to a company that makes them feel fulfilled in their work.

PEOPLE WANT TO BE CONNECTED TO ORGANIZATIONS THAT VALUE THEM, GIVE THEM IMPORTANT WORK TO DO, AND TREAT THEM WITH RESPECT.

In addition, Ritz Carlton's employees all are empowered to make decisions to ensure that guests are satisfied. When you talk to them about a problem, they don't pass the buck to the manager. Instead, they immediately take ownership of the problem and deal with it, then follow up afterward. That attitude is apparent in their credo, "We are ladies and gentlemen serving ladies and gentlemen."

It's about value, respect, and significance. Why do some companies in Silicon Valley have no trouble attracting people in spite of that area's talent shortage? It's because people want to be connected to organizations that value them, give them important work to do, and treat them with respect.

---

3. Mark Morrison, "Herb Kelleher on the Record, Part 2," *BusinessWeek*, December 23, 2003.

TAKING APPROPRIATE ACTION

As a leader, you need many different kinds of people around you, and often, problems arise when you're unsure of how to engage and disengage with them. I've found it helpful to determine whom I can help grow as a leader, who can grow alongside me, and who can help me develop my own leadership potential.

And since all people are different, we engage each of them differently. We either (1) reach down to those below us, whom we can assist; (2) reach out to those around us, who are where we are presently; or (3) reach up to those above us, who are where we want to be.

First, leaders are people who share what they've learned with others. They use their own growth to help others to grow, and they purposefully mentor others. When we grow others, we also grow ourselves.

Furthermore, a leader does three things: They know, they grow, and they show. Knowing involves getting information. By

WHEN WE GROW OTHERS, WE ALSO GROW OURSELVES.

using the information you acquire, you grow and develop yourself. But that alone doesn't make you a leader—you have to show someone else what you know.

Giving away what you've learned sounds odd. Why would you share your hard-earned secrets with someone else? Because the best use of your power is empowering others. You never lose by giving away power. When you empower someone else, you've made a friend for life.

YOU NEVER LOSE BY GIVING AWAY POWER. WHEN YOU EMPOWER SOMEONE ELSE, YOU'VE MADE A FRIEND FOR LIFE.

In addition, we reach out to those around us, who are where we are presently. If both your company and your friend's company have one hundred trucks, the two of you can commiserate about your troubles and rejoice in your successes. During this conversation, you both are learning from each other's experience. You may not be adding a lot of value to each other, but you're creating cohesiveness, camaraderie, and collegiality by being transparent with each other.

Last, we reach up to those above us, who are where we want to be. It's important that we also get their assistance. Put yourself in places to be recognized, and let these people know that you'd like to learn from their knowledge and experience.

DISENGAGING FROM PEOPLE IS DIFFICULT— IT'S PAINFUL AND MESSY.

This last category can be somewhat painful. That's because you may have to disengage with people who have brought you where you are in order to engage with people who can take you forward. If you've been spending time with a new group of people, you won't have time to devote to the people you used to see. If your company is growing, you will

be busy engaging with people running other growing companies. You won't have to spend with the people who run small
companies.

Disengaging from people
is difficult—it's painful and
messy. It's painful because you
may really care about these
people and do not want to disengage from them. But unless

**LEADERS GROW ONLY
TO THE THRESHOLD OF
THEIR PAIN.**

you disengage, you won't have time to engage with new people.
It's also painful to realize that we may never see these two different groups of people together because their worlds and realities are so different. And people you're disengaging from will
not always be able to understand why. It's painful all the way
around. But, remember, unless you are willing to endure these
pains, your own growth as a leader will be limited. Leaders
grow only to the threshold of their pain.

TEACHING POINTS

1. All leaders need new people in their lives. The people
   who get us where we are may not be the ones who will
   take us where we need to go.

2. Many difficulties we encounter come from not knowing how to deal with issues and situations raised by
   different types of people.

3. We'll encounter people who agree and disagree
   with us. Agreement is not always positive, and

disagreement is not always negative. People can disagree with us and still add value to our church or organization.

4. We'll have to deal with people we've outgrown or outpaced.

5. People who are tied to yesterday's solutions can become today's problems.

6. There are also people who will stay only within the boundaries of their job description and will not take ownership of situations.

7. A leader must deal with static people and static organizations. When they're not moving in sync, there is a lack of organizational congruence.

8. During their first ninety days of work, new workers can often offer us new perspectives and shed light on redundancies and ineffectiveness.

9. As we rise in leadership, there will be few people who understand the reality of our position. So it's important to find people we can be transparent with about our struggles and concerns.

10. We should also surround ourselves with people who can celebrate our successes without being jealous or envious.

11. We need different types of people in our lives. As we focus on growing people, our organization will

experience growth. Areas of growth include competency, character, and chemistry.

12. We must surround ourselves with people who will challenge us. If we hire only people like us, we will never complement our weaknesses within the organization.

13. As long as our organization shows workers that they are valued by giving them important work to do and treating them with respect, we'll never experience a talent shortage.

14. When interacting with people, we should:

    a. Reach down to those who are where we used to be.

    b. Reach out to peers who are where we are presently.

    c. Reach up to those who are where we'd like to be.

15. Unless we're willing to engage with new people and disengage with others, our own leadership growth will be limited.

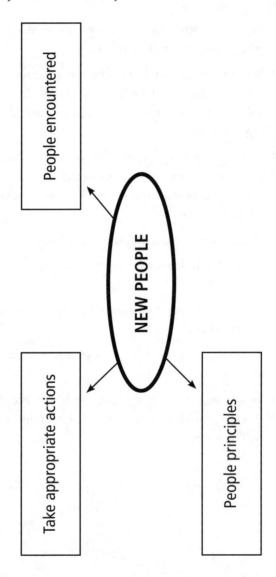

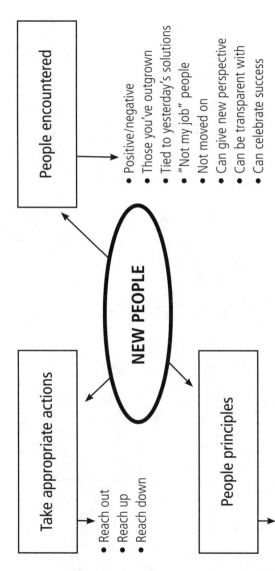

People encountered

- Positive/negative
- Those you've outgrown
- Tied to yesterday's solutions
- "Not my job" people
- Not moved on
- Can give new perspective
- Can be transparent with
- Can celebrate success

NEW PEOPLE

Take appropriate actions

- Reach out
- Reach up
- Reach down

People principles

- Grow others
- Focus on organizational context
- Staff your weaknesses

2

NEW PAINS

"God whispers to us in our pleasures, speaks in
our conscience, but shouts in our pains: it is His
megaphone to rouse a deaf world."[4]
—C. S. Lewis

After the front door closed behind her, Jill dropped her
briefcase, switched on the living-room light, and sank wearily
into her favorite armchair. Leaving for work in the dark and
coming home after sunset was becoming a routine. With local
fire codes forcing the center to turn away increasing numbers
of needy families, she continued an uphill battle to expand the
facility to meet the needs of the community.

At the end of yet another long day, she wondered if the
expansion strategy was taking the center one step forward
and two steps back. After weeks of frustrating paperwork and
endless board meetings, she had finally put the grant proposals for the needed funds into the hands of the government
decision makers. But she now awaited news of the proposals

---

4. C. S. Lewis, *The Problem of Pain* (New York: HarperOne), 91.

without the much-needed support of her assistant director, Ann.

Together, Ann and Jill had raised the funds to start the center, and they had enthusiastically championed its activities. But almost as soon as the new expansion plans had begun, Ann began calling in sick and became increasingly critical of the expansion. Jill had finally asked for Ann's resignation after weeks of painful conversations and her own internal debates.

Taking a pile of resumes from her briefcase, Jill wondered why she hadn't seen the signs of Ann's descent earlier, and she hoped she could locate a replacement to help her manage the expansion.

Today's leaders are feeling pains they've never felt before. Explosive change is causing some of these pains. For example, organization must survive rapid technological innovation, losing honest and competent people, and operating in different cultures. Pastors must face the pains of misplaced leaders, building programs, growing or lagging membership, and abundant or lacking resources.

The increased rate of change gives everything a shorter shelf life. Not long ago, when a person got a job, he or she was content to work there until retiring with a gold Rolex. Now, it's estimated that Generation Xers will make job changes every three to five years, while Millennials will do so even more often.[5] And people are relocating as often as they're changing

5. Doug and Polly White, "What to Expect from Gen-X and Millennial Employees," *Entrepreneur*, December 23, 2014, http://www.entrepreneur.com/article/240556.

jobs, with the average American projected to live in 11.7 houses in 2013.[6]

However, change isn't the only cause of our pains. The higher your position, the more pains you will have to bear. If you went to graduate school, for example, you

TODAY'S LEADERS ARE FEELING PAINS THEY'VE NEVER FELT BEFORE.

probably have endured pains that someone with a high school diploma has never encountered. If you're the local mayor, your pains come from being kept accountable, critiqued, and criticized by the people of your town. When you become governor, you will have even more pains. If you rise from governor to president, you will have some *major* pains!

Many people don't seek public office because they're unwilling to put up with the pains of those positions. We all have thresholds of pain—both consciously and unconsciously—that cause us to say, "That's not worth it." When you're the CEO, you're never "off." You may be out of the office, but you're always on call. You have pains that most people will never understand.

Think about the number of people who wish they could be Bill Gates. There's no shortage of people dreaming of being one of the wealthiest men in the world, or imagining their picture on the cover of *Time* as "Man of the Year." They don't think

6. Mona Chalabi, "How Many Times Does the Average American Move?" *FiveThirtyEight*, January 29, 2015, http://fivethirtyeight.com/datalab/how-many-times-the-average-person-moves/.

WHEN YOU'RE THE CEO, YOU'RE NEVER "OFF."

about the price Bill Gates paid or the pains he endured. For example, they don't imagine themselves being in his shoes during the Microsoft antitrust trial. They didn't aspire to be the Microsoft CEO when his proposal to merge companies had been turned down by AOL, which afterward announced its partnership with his rival, Google. They don't realize that Bill Gates became Man of the Year for his philanthropic work, not for creating Microsoft. They've never imagined his pains.

NECESSARY PAINS

Now some pains are quite normal. Scripture tells us not be surprised or dismayed by the *"fiery ordeal*[s]*"* (1 Peter 4:12) we encounter. As leaders, we should accept certain pains as part of the job; they just come with the territory.

Obviously, I'm not referring to the pains of wrongdoing or the pains of injury or illness. I'm talking about the pains that come as you begin fulfilling your vision, which can be compared to the pains of childbirth—they are not pleasant, they bring much discomfort and distress, but these pains seem relatively small in the grander scheme, compared to what is to come.

Often, pains come with the painstaking efforts and great care and diligence we invest in our work.. To grow as a leader, we must be willing to embrace them. In fact, our willingness to handle pains will determine the level of leadership to which we'll rise.

I know some great preachers who will always pastor small churches simply because they cannot handle the issues and challenges that would come with larger ones. Then there are other pastors who will end up in larger churches because they are more capable of handling pain. They may not be as talented as the small-church pastor, but they have a higher pain threshold.

> **OUR WILLINGNESS TO HANDLE PAINS WILL DETERMINE THE LEVEL OF LEADERSHIP TO WHICH WE'LL RISE.**

For example, if you leave a nine-to-five job to start a fast-food franchise, you will face all kinds of new pains. Working longer hours will challenge your family life. If the business continues to grow, you might think about starting another franchise, which will bring another level of pain. Some people wouldn't consider opening a second franchise; others wouldn't even consider opening the first one. To them, it wouldn't even be worth it. It would be just too painful.

VARIETIES OF PAIN

The force of a bullet strikes you like a sledgehammer, knocking you backward. Your windows vibrate at the rumble of distant thunder. Storm clouds are approaching. Pains come at many levels. What types of pains do leaders typically experience?

At various times, they'll encounter:

+ *Internal pain.* These are the bullets that come as you deal with various internal struggles, such as realizing our inadequacies, rising to the level of our incompetence, and disengaging from familiar people.

+ *External pain.* These pains are the approaching storm clouds. They tend to have outside causes, such as cultural changes, external pressures, and competitive realities.

+ *Organizational pain.* As you respond to external realities, you'll find yourself dealing with organizational conflict, and making decisions that involve increasingly higher stakes.

Internal Pain

Realizing our inadequacies. It happens. Despite our best research and preparation, things don't turn out as we expect. It's easy to begin to question our own competency, mission, and judgment, especially when we hear the loud voices of our critics.

Oftentimes, we lay awake, listening to our loudest critic—ourselves—ask us questions in the dark. "Why didn't I do that?" "Why did I make that choice?" Our own inadequacies bring pain.

Rising to the level of our incompetence. Every leader has his own glass ceiling, the place that he just can't move beyond. Eventually, all of us reach a glass ceiling, or the level of our incompetence, as described by the Peter Principle.

Maybe you've realized that you can't grow your church beyond 200 people. You average between 180 and 220 congregants, bumping up and down. It doesn't matter what you do, that's where you remain.

Or perhaps your organization is stalled. Despite your research into new markets and new product launches, you can't take it

EMERGING FROM A PAINFUL LEVEL IS POSSIBLE.

any further. A growth strategy seems to elude you. It's a painful place to be.

However, if we're willing to challenge our own thinking, as described in the chapter 4, "New Perspectives," we can emerge from this stagnation.

Disengaging from familiar people. This is always painful. A number of times, I've had to part ways with or let go of people who have accompanied me on my journey. I've hired a lot of people, and I've fired a lot of people, too. It raises questions about loyalty, entitlement, friendship; and it's always painful. I hurt for people.

Separations are often unavoidable business realities. When Delta Airlines filed for bankruptcy, it had to let thousands of people go. The company couldn't keep doing

SEPARATIONS ARE OFTEN UNAVOIDABLE BUSINESS REALITIES.

business as usual. As part of their restructuring, Ford also cut thousands of jobs. It's never an easy decision.

LETTING GO OF PEOPLE CREATES ALL KINDS OF PAINS.

Pastors know the pain of separation, too. It's particularly painful when it involves good, faithful people. As one pastor said, "One woman was our first Sunday-school teacher. One man has been my deacon and my organist since we were twenty-five years old. They always gave sacrificially and hung in there with us. But now we need someone who can take us to another level."

Letting go of people creates all kinds of pains, but making those changes is frequently a requirement to moving forward. This pain is part of the challenge of leadership.

Finding new qualified people. A growing organization needs new talented people. The challenge of finding these people brings new pain.

There are the pains of deciding what type of skills, characteristics, certifications, and education are required, then conducting interviews to determine which person has the right mix of competency, character, and chemistry to fit in with your organization. And there is also additional pain if we're filling the position of someone we just let go.

Inability to articulate internal realities. Developing a vision can be a very intuitive, creative process. While the vision is percolating inside our heart and our spirit, we know something exciting is happening. Early in that process, it's hard to synchronize our minds and words with what we see.

I've seen this a lot with leaders, especially with pastors. They have an inspiring, exciting idea about where they want to go. Many times, they find it difficult to articulate; and

IT'S HARD TO SYNCHRONIZE OUR MINDS AND WORDS WITH WHAT WE SEE.

when they do attempt to express it, sometimes it's vague, general, and amorphous—even to them! That's a frustrating and painful place to be.

External Pain

Changing cultural norms. The changing cultural norms of today and tomorrow raise questions about how to get things done. It doesn't matter how slowly or quickly a familiar cultural landscape is transformed into an unfamiliar seascape, it still creates pains.

For example, the hierarchical culture of the boss telling employees what to do has fallen by the wayside and is being replaced by a collaborative culture of consensus building. No longer is it enough for a CEO on the eighteenth floor to send a directive. Now he must get a buy-in from the vice presidents, who get a buy-in from the managers, who get a buy-in from the supervisors and foremen, who get a buy-in from the people on the floor. Tom Friedman talks about this in *The World Is Flat*; the hierarchies, pyramids, and flowcharts that once described how things got done do not work anymore.

CULTURAL SHIFTS DEMAND NEW WAYS OF LOOKING AT THINGS AND NEW VOCABULARIES.

Cultural shifts demand new ways of looking at things and new vocabularies. Virtual teams, collaborative groups, and task forces are emphasized in this new language. Products are marketed in entirely new ways. Delta Airlines is marketing Starbucks. Starbucks is marketing *The Atlanta Journal Constitution*. Rented movies are advertising TV programs, and TV programs are advertising websites. Everything is more tightly interwoven.

There's a new team with new delivery systems integrating the vertical smokestacks of yesterday. In times past, the majority of business was transacted locally, so if you weren't in Atlanta, we wouldn't work together. Now, cell phones, e-mail, and digital networks have tied people together from across the globe. For example, I live in Atlanta, Georgia, my ghostwriter lives in northern New Jersey, and this book was published in New Kensington, Pennsylvania.

While new delivery systems provide new capabilities, they cause pains, as well. For example, when scheduling multinational conference calls, what time zone gets preference? And when transacting commerce, what exchange rate do you use? That's part of transitioning to new cultural norms.

Changing external realities. The pace of progress demands faster and more proactive action. This frantic pace brings with it the realization that—despite your intensive market analysis, demographic studies,

THE PACE OF PROGRESS DEMANDS FASTER AND MORE PROACTIVE ACTION.

and strategic plans—you're no longer in the driver's seat with both hands firmly on the wheel.

Sometimes, the realization comes slowly. A local expansion widens a roadway, displacing smaller and older businesses with new ones. Perhaps one of them was one of your dependable suppliers, which forces you to find a replacement. This leads to even more change, especially if that road construction happens to be making room for a new superstore.

It's painful to realize your lack of influence over issues and situations you once had control of.

Competitive realities. Competitive landscapes can quickly become raging seascapes, capable of swallowing even the most legendary organizations.

Remember when AT&T was the only game in town? First, threats came from Sprint, MCI, and other long-distance companies. Then, more intense competition grew from the Baby Bells, which were once part of the AT&T family. Finally, the competitive environment was completely altered when cell-phone, cable TV, and Internet companies started providing inexpensive calling plans. And now the cycle is beginning again.

Certainly, the pains of remaining relevant or competitive are no picnic; but paying attention to those pains can keep you from becoming irrelevant or an acquisition target or even a statistic.

Organizational Pain

Internal organizational conflict. A small organization experiences relatively little strife. Smaller numbers make it easier to manage expectations and minimize conflict when people's expectations differ from their experience.

As your organization becomes more successful and your staff expands, it's tougher to manage the conflict between people's expectations and reality. You also have to contend with staff-related competition and different perspectives, preferences, and biases. Indeed, the success of a growing organization brings new pain.

THE SUCCESS OF A GROWING ORGANIZATION BRINGS NEW PAIN.

Decisions with higher stakes. When I became president of Beulah Heights Bible College, our entire annual budget was under $100,000. Eventually, we progressed to million-dollar budgets. Every decision I made involved increasingly higher stakes. I was constantly aware that making a bad decision could result in a significant revenue loss or affect the job security of the ninety-three employees. The stress of making high-priority, life-and-death decisions is what

THE ANGST OF THE STRUGGLE TO MAKE THE RIGHT DECISION ALWAYS BRINGS PAINS.

ages US presidents; they enter the White House looking young and come out with gray hair and bags under their eyes. It's because every stroke counts significantly.

Now my pains are different. A bad business decision would affect only my family, my assistant, and me. It's much different than it was when I was president of the college, when my decisions affected the lives of many more people. The angst of making the right decision is always painful.

Transformational Pain

When Lou Gerstner became the chairman and CEO of IBM in 1993, the company was in trouble. During his first meeting, the leadership team discussed IBM's strategy. When that eight-hour meeting ended, Gerstner said he didn't understand a thing; it was almost as if the other leaders spoke a different language.

That meeting, as painful as it was, revealed to him exactly what he was up against in making the company profitable. Eventually, he had to transform IBM's powerful culture, which made it both famous and successful in the 1960s and '70s.

Imagine being a company outsider and having to transform an icon like IBM. How did he do it? Gerstner made friends with his pains. He embraced the pain of transforming the famous IBM culture, the pain of centralizing what had become a very individualistic operation, and the pain of flying in the face of many other things that were considered standard operating procedure. By embracing these pains, he turned IBM around.

Athletes must embrace their pain, too. They are always playing while hurting. They know they have to make friends with their pain. One professional athlete said that playing football was like "being in a car wreck every day."[7] Why did he continue doing it? Because he loved it; he understood that his pain was the price he had to pay.

ALL LEADERS MUST BEAR THE PAINS OF CRITICISM.

Likewise, leaders must embrace their pain, tough it is never easy. And all leaders must bear the pain of criticism. You cannot be a leader and avoid it. Everything the president of the United States says and does is intensely scrutinized. Talk-show hosts love to dissect his policies and actions. It takes thick skin to be the president.

When Princess Camilla visited America, the press criticized her for what she wore and what she didn't wear. They

---

7. "The Painful Lives of Football Players," ABC News, http://abcnews.go.com/GMA/ESPNSports/story?id=1528986&CMP=OTC-RSSFeeds0312.

wrote about how many changes of clothes she brought for an eight-day visit. Imagine being Camilla and reading an article that said she looked "frumpy." That's painful. But if you want to be a princess or a president, that's what you have to deal with.

Making friends with your pain is a part of leadership. It tells us that we are moving in the right direction. So we must accept that pain will always be a part of our life as we continue climbing the ladder to our destiny.

NEW PAIN WILL ALWAYS BE A PART OF YOUR LIFE AS WE CONTINUE CLIMBING THE LADDER TO OUR DESTINY.

TEACHING POINTS

1. The quick rate of change is causing new pains, giving everything a shorter shelf life.

2. The higher our position, the more pains we must bear.

3. Our willingness to handle pain determines the level of leadership to which we'll rise.

4. We'll encounter internal pain, external pain, and organizational pain.

   a. Internal pain arises from realizing our own personal inadequacies, rising to the level of our incompetence, disengaging from familiar people, finding new qualified people, and being unable to articulate internal realities.

i. Despite our best efforts, things may not turn out as expected, causing us to question our choices.

ii. We may reach a level that we simply cannot move beyond.

iii. Separation from people we know is often an unavoidable but painful reality.

iv. We also experience the pains of needing and finding the right people.

v. Inability to express our vision can also be painful.

b. External pain comes from changing cultural norms, a lack of control over external realities, and competitive pressures.

i. Changing cultural norms raise questions about how we should get things done.

ii. We lack control over issues and situations we want to control, and we lose control over things we once controlled.

iii. Competitive landscapes can quickly be transformed into raging seascapes.

   c.   Organizational pain includes organizational conflict and decision-making with higher stakes.

       i.   As an organization grows, it becomes more difficult to manage expectations and minimize conflict.

      ii.   Rising in leadership requires difficult decision-making, which involves larger budgets and affects many more people.

5.   Embracing pain is a necessary part of leadership.

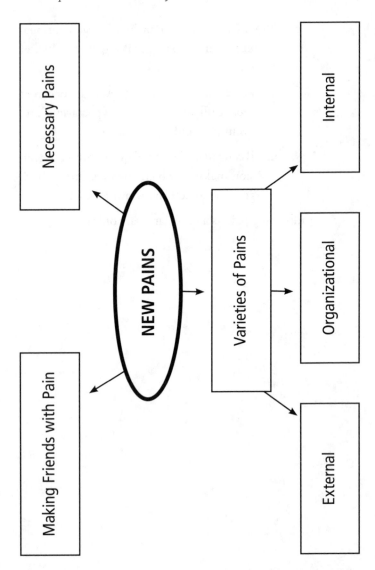

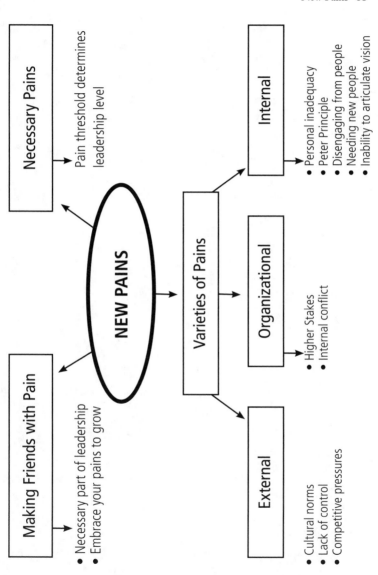

Making Friends with Pain
→ • Necessary part of leadership
• Embrace your pains to grow

Necessary Pains
→ Pain threshold determines leadership level

NEW PAINS

Varieties of Pains

External
→ • Cultural norms
• Lack of control
• Competitive pressures

Organizational
→ • Higher Stakes
• Internal conflict

Internal
→ • Personal inadequacy
• Peter Principle
• Disengaging from people
• Needing new people
• Inability to articulate vision

3

NEW PLACES

"The next sea change is upon us. We must recognize
this change as an opportunity to take our offerings to
the next level...."[8]
—Bill Gates

B*logging.* Until a few weeks ago, Jill had never heard the term.
Since the board's recent decision to use this new Internet technology to publicize her non-profit group's activities, she's read
and talked about little else. Apparently, keeping a blog—which
is short for "Weblog"—was the latest high-tech business tool.
Written in an informal style, almost like an online diary, blogs
can give any organization—including big companies like GM
and Google—a more human voice.

Jill had hoped her forays into the strange land of technology were over when she launched the group's website. Now, she
puzzled over how a blog would connect people with their char-
itable work in the community, and wondered where she'd find

8. Memo of Bill Gates quoted in Mary Jo Foley, "Gates Memo: We've Got to
Get This Services Thing Right," *PC Magazine*, November 9, 2005, http://
www.pcmag.com/article2/0,2817,1884289,00.asp.

the talent to keep the content fresh and interesting. Smiling to herself, she thought about one of the kids who lived a few floors down, and how he could probably wrap up this blog thing much more quickly and capably.

Church and business leaders around the world are finding themselves in brand-new places due to the needs arising in their communities. They may or may not be writing blogs, but they are reaching out in ways that, just a few years earlier, had not even been on their radar. They are moving to new places with their products, with their mode of delivery, and with their customer service.

Moving to new places is good. The American Indians understood this. If they didn't like someone, they'd curse him by saying, "May you stay in the same place." They were obviously referring to more than just geography. They were wishing that person a stagnant personal journey, a family that wouldn't grow, a future that wouldn't prosper. They were wishing that he would remain in the same condition, without movement, growth, and change.

REMAINING IN THE SAME PLACE PRODUCES MEDIOCRITY.

Remaining in the same place produces mediocrity. Many years ago, farmers discovered that when land was forced to produce the same crops year after year, the soil was robbed of its essential nutrients. In the days before fertilizer, to continue producing good crops, farmers would change locations of their crops or let a piece of farmland rest for a season, giving the soil a chance to renew itself. Change was regarded as a good and necessary thing.

THE JOURNEY TO NEW PLACES

A leader's nature is to seek out and journey to new places. In order to do so, a leader must:

+ Develop a clear vision of his destination.

+ Disengage with activities and people not headed in that direction.

+ Connect with people who are at his desired destination.

A clear vision is a necessity. Once your destination is clear, you're more inclined to find the resources that can take you where you want to go. For instance, the

A CLEAR VISION IS A NECESSITY.

vision of growing a business that develops websites with safe online shopping will drive your thinking and your activities. You won't allow yourself to be sidetracked by seminars for video-game developers or industry associations for shoe salesmen.

I'm finding that more and more leaders have clearer visions of their destinations. They define where they want to go and investing resources that will take them there.

However, a clear vision is not the only requirement for reaching your destination. Some leaders know that they want to go west, for example, but they linger at the eastern seaboard.

Occasionally, they gaze at the train headed for the frontier they've been dreaming of.

No amount of wishing, dreaming, or visioning is ever going to get them where they want to go. Reaching their destination requires that they first disengage from the people in their lives and the place they're at so they can catch the train headed in the right direction.

How important is disengaging? Disengaging was probably what maintained Intel's profitability—and possibly their existence—in the extremely competitive chip market.

In the early 1980s, most of Intel's top executives didn't see the need to change a thing. At the time, it was probably the leading provider of memory chips and was making about one billion dollars a year.

DON'T THINK THAT DISENGAGING IS EASY. CEO Gordon Moore knew that the industry would have to undergo drastic changes, because Japanese firms were starting to manufacture the same chips at such a low cost that they would soon become commodities. By 1984, Intel's profits fell below two million.[9]

Don't think that disengaging is easy. In his book *Only the Paranoid Survive: How to Identify and Exploit the Crisis Points*

9. Richard S. Tedlow, "The Education of Andy Grove," *Fortune*, December 12, 2005, http://archive.fortune.com/magazines/fortune/fortune_archive/2005/12/12/8363124/index.htm.

That Challenge Every Business, Andrew Grove says that he knew that Intel had to exit that market but had trouble even getting the words out of his mouth. Over time, he was able to take the necessary, painful decision of disengaging from the market that Intel had virtually created so they could move forward. Disengaging was painful all around for Intel. It meant layoffs for thousands of employees and the company's first loss since its start-up days.

Was it worth it? Let's answer one question with another: Does the slogan "Intel Inside" mean anything to you? Disengaging from the memory chip market

YOU CANNOT REMAIN STATIC IF YOU WANT TO KEEP MOVING.

enabled Intel to focus on developing a new and faster microprocessor that would power IBM's new personal computer. The rest—as they say—is history. But the first step in getting there was disengaging.

You cannot remain static if you want to keep moving. You have to become a part of something that is moving and associate with people who are moving. And if your church, company, or organization is going somewhere, you'll find that people will want to be connected with you, so that they can go somewhere, too.

In addition to connecting yourself to people and organizations that are moving, it's important to identify, connect with, and seek help from people who are already at your destination.

Talking with people who are where you want to go helps you to develop a much clearer vision of your destination.

COPING ON THE JOURNEY

TALKING WITH PEOPLE WHO ARE WHERE YOU WANT TO GO HELPS YOU TO DEVELOP A MUCH CLEARER VISION OF YOUR DESTINATION.

A journey to a new place can be uncomfortable because you have to leave the familiar, your comfort zone, and travel into the unknown.

While there may be no maps of your new location, there are four principles that can help you navigate the terrain of any unfamiliar territory:

- Be ready to give up the familiar to make friends with the unfamiliar.

- Be comfortable with ambiguity.

- Be flexible with your direction.

EVERYTHING IN OUR PSYCHE WANTS TO STAY IN THE FAMILIAR; EVERYTHING IN GOD'S PSYCHE WANTS TO MOVE US TO THE UNFAMILIAR.

Anytime we journey into the unfamiliar, we will experience a certain amount of concern, angst, and nervousness. When God asks us to go to new places, we have to give up the familiar and *make friends with the unfamiliar.* Everything in our psyche wants to stay in the familiar; everything in God's psyche wants to move us to the unfamiliar.

Scripture is full of examples of this. God said, "Abraham, you're familiar with this land, but I'm taking you into a land that you haven't seen." (See Genesis 12:1.)

"David, you're familiar with the sheep, but I'm going to take you into the unfamiliar territory of kingship and politics."

"Daniel, you are familiar with working in high levels of government, but I'm going to take you into the unfamiliar place of taking a stand for righteousness."

"Peter, you're a good fisherman, but I'm going to make you a fisher of men." (See Matthew 4:19; Mark 1:17.)

IT'S IN THE UNCERTAIN, THE UNFAMILIAR, AND THE NEW PLACES THAT WE TRUST GOD IN NEW WAYS.

While everything in us wants to stay in the known and the familiar, God is always trying to take us toward the uncertain and unfamiliar, because that's where we trust God in new ways.

In addition to becoming comfortable with your journey to new places, we have to create an organizational culture that will make friends with the unfamiliar, a culture that fosters innovative thinking and is open to exploring new ideas and traveling to new places. Too many organizations reward employees only for keeping with what's familiar.

Two years before Netscape Communications launched the first Web browser, a researcher showed a prototype to Hewlett-Packard's CEO. Now, the CEO was excited about the browser concept and passed it along to the leaders of HP's computer division. But when the computer division reviewed the browser, they rejected it. Why? Partly because they couldn't imagine how this new thing could help sell computers, and partly because management always stressed the importance of meeting quarterly goals over investing in new programs.

Failing to make friends with the unfamiliar can be costly. While your organization needs processes, you have to be careful that you're not stifling innovative thinking that could take you to unfamiliar places.

Google is a great example of a company that nurtures innovation. All their engineers are given one day a week to work solely on their own pet projects, even if they don't directly relate to the company's efforts. If their jobs prevent them from using this independent time, they can save it up and use it later. Their top executives also have office hours dedicated to discussing new ideas with employees. And any employee can post new ideas for the business and discuss them on their online bulletin boards.

Google knows that in order for their organization to grow, they must get comfortable with the unfamiliar. You have to be willing to move into uncertainty and willing to venture into unknown territory. For example, suppose your organization has always done well with one person handling your bookkeeping. As you grow, however, it becomes too much work for just one or two people, so your lead bookkeeper proposes an outsourcing arrangement. At first, you might not be comfortable with the new proposal. You enjoy directly overseeing his work, knowing how he does things, and you enjoy walking down the hall to his office and asking questions. You wouldn't know these new accountants, so it would be uncomfortable; but to walk into growth, you must be willing to walk into the unfamiliar.

Every leader also has to *be comfortable with ambiguity*, both real and perceived. We like to think that we know where we're going, but all we really have is a general direction.

TO WALK INTO GROWTH, YOU MUST BE WILLING TO WALK INTO THE UNFAMILIAR.

We are always living with the ambiguous. We probably have many questions we'd like to answer, but we just have to see what happens as the journey unfolds. You have to accept that some issues can be solved only as you move forward. Once you reach one milestone, you'll have other things to figure out. Your destination is always perceived; it hasn't yet become a reality. You may have mapped out your strategy and developed some tactics, but as your journey unfolds, situations will change in ways you could not have perceived beforehand.

Because things change during your journey, you also have to be flexible with your direction. Having the flexibility to make midcourse corrections and shift lanes is an important part of reaching your destination.

My own destination has been distilling itself over time. I came to America as a student and became the breakfast cook, dishwasher, and janitor at my college. After I graduated, I became the assistant pastor of a church, got married, started a family, and then became the senior pastor. Then I became president of Beulah Heights Bible College (now Beulah Heights University) and later its chancellor. Now I'm writing books, speaking, and consulting. I've had to become comfortable with shifting lanes and making transitions. If my uneasiness had kept me from shifting lanes, I would have gotten "arthritis of life" and gotten stuck somewhere along the way.

Have you ever noticed people who stay in the passing lane on the highway? I don't ever want to stay in that lane, because getting to new places sometimes means getting off at an exit, taking a detour, and getting back on the expressway farther down the road. Finding new places also requires a certain amount of *flexibility*.

Don't underestimate the importance of making friends with the unfamiliar, being comfortable with ambiguity, and staying flexible. These are critical principles to master, for you're not a pioneer traveling across land in a covered wagon—you're the captain of a sailboat navigating the changing and uncharted waters of the sea. Watching the ocean from a beach reminds us that the land we're standing on is stationary and static. However, just a few feet ahead, the sea changes every second.

EXPECT TO NAVIGATE THE SEA AND NOT LAND

Transformed leaders know they must operate on the sea and not land. Why? Because their journey will not take them through a stationary environment but a dynamic and ever-changing one. Unpreparedness for a dynamic environment causes problems for many organizations.

Consider AT&T. For years, the company monopolized the telecommunications industry. Even after parts of the business had been broken

LEADERS EMPHASIZE THE SEA OVER THE LAND.

up into regional telephone companies, the leaders continued to operate like the monopoly they had been for so many years. They were not able to shift lanes because they still thought like a huge behemoth. In many ways, they behaved as if they were living on land while they were really on the shifting sea.

Delta Airlines is another example. They faced financial trouble while cut-rate providers—like Air Tran, Southwest, Frontier, and others—were making money, partly because were smaller and nimbler. So Delta Airlines started scanning the environment and adapting to the evolving conditions around them, and they continue to do so. When the land changes into a sea, they are willing to adapt and change quickly. They are like little sports cars, weaving in and out of traffic, not large tractor-trailers.

In *The World Is Flat: A Brief History of the Twenty-First Century*, Tom Friedman talks about the effects of globalization. He makes the point that while many things in the global economy have changed quite rapidly, our delivery systems and methodologies have not. We have to be willing to make changes as we navigate the sea, because it changes every second. We always have to be open to new places and be willing to catch the next wave.

WE HAVE TO BE WILLING TO MAKE CHANGES AS WE NAVIGATE THE SEA, BECAUSE IT CHANGES EVERY SECOND.

No organization is immune to this. Don't think that because your church is healthy, it doesn't need to change. Reflecting on his ten-year anniversary of becoming pastor of First Evangelical Free Church, H. Dale Burke observed that healthy churches have a harder time seeing the need to change. No one may be very concerned about subtle symptoms of falling behind at a healthy church. But that doesn't mean that changes aren't needed to reach a changing world.[10]

Knowing that we're navigating a sea provides us with some important information:

+ The environment is always changing.

+ It's changing faster than we realize.

+ We all are going to new places.

---

10. H. Dale Burke, "Even Healthy Churches Need to Change," *Leadership Journal*, Fall 2005, http://www.christianitytoday.com/le/2005/fall/3.43.html.

+ We should be thinking about those new places so that we can change our trajectory as needed to reach our destination.

You'd better believe that Bill Gates closely watched the sea changes affecting his industry and adjusted his route to reach his destination. In 2005, to lead Microsoft into the next phase of change brought on by the Internet, he hired a new chief technical officer, Ray Ozzie. At the time, Microsoft already head been anticipating changes in how software would be distributed, used, and paid for, changes that might resemble the peer-to-peer technology model that Napster made popular.[11]Bill Gates watched for sea changes for quite some time. In a memo titled "The Internet Tidal Wave," written in 1995, he had forecasted how the Internet would alter the computing industry and what it would mean for Microsoft. Bill Gates paid attention to the sea; he knew that if he rode the waves, they would take him and his company to new places.

TEACHING POINTS

1. Going to new places is a good and necessary thing. Remaining in the same place only produces mediocrity.

2. Reaching new places requires developing a clear vision of our destination, disengaging with people and activities not headed in that direction, and connecting with people who are headed to our destination.

---

11. Steve Lohr, "Can This Man Reprogram Microsoft?" *New York Times*, December 11, 2005, http://www.nytimes.com/2005/12/11/business/yourmoney/can-this-man-reprogram-microsoft.html?_r=0.

> a. Once our destination is clear, we're more inclined to find the necessary resources.
>
> b. Reaching our destination involves disengaging from where we are presently. We cannot remain static.
>
> c. We must also connect with people who are already where we want to go.

3. Going to new places is easier when we make friends with the unfamiliar, are comfortable with ambiguity, and remain flexible.

4. Leaders expect to navigate the sea and not land.

5. Human nature does not want to part with the familiar, but we have to be ready to leave our comfort zone and journey into the unknown.

6. We have to create organizational cultures that foster innovative thinking. Failing to do this can be costly.

7. We always live with the ambiguous, even though we like to think we know where we're headed.

8. Situations and circumstances often change, so we have to remain flexible enough to make course corrections.

9. We must be ready to catch the next wave, because things change faster than we realize.

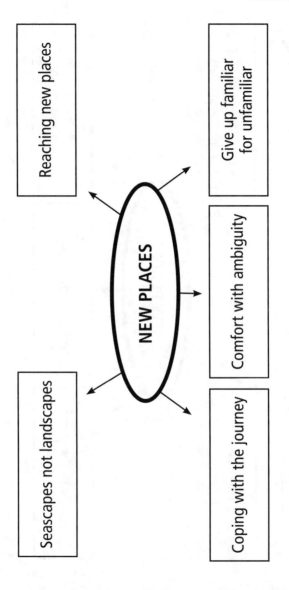

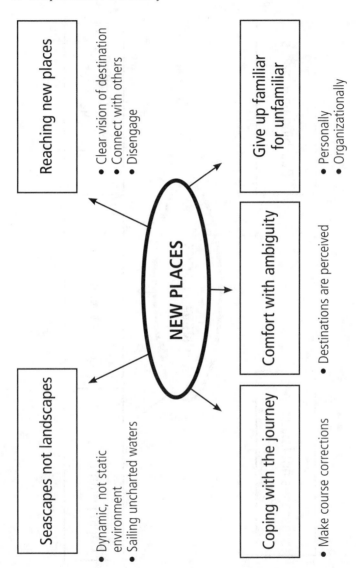

Reaching new places

- Clear vision of destination
- Connect with others
- Disengage

Give up familiar for unfamiliar

- Personally
- Organizationally

NEW PLACES

Comfort with ambiguity

- Destinations are perceived

Seascapes not landscapes

- Dynamic, not static environment
- Sailing uncharted waters

Coping with the journey

- Make course corrections

4

NEW PERSPECTIVES

"He not busy being born is busy dying."[12]
—Bob Dylan

The glowing digital clock signaled 3 A.M. Unable to sleep, youth pastor Joe quietly tiptoed downstairs, unplugged his guitar from its amp, and strummed quietly. Across town, senior pastor Jake Barrett mentally revisited the same board meeting as his youth pastor.

Joe's quiet energy and passion had invigorated the church's teen and college-aged youth. Still, the board had been divided over his proposal for a Friday-night youth service, voicing concern that an evening gathering would deplete Sunday morning attendance. Joe had described similar gatherings that had increased overall interest in spiritual matters, but the board hadn't budged.

Staring at his guitar, Joe wondered why no amount of information seemed to sway the board members, why they refused to even experiment.

12. Bob Dylan, "It's Alright, Ma (I'm Only Bleeding)," 1965.

In his kitchen, Jake questioned his own reservations, asking himself why he'd resisted Joe's new idea, when he had renewed the interest of the church youth.

As the clock glowed 4 A.M., both men sat pondering in silence.

Every leader needs to be able to see things differently, to think outside the box. The business world values fresh perspectives, because being different, being ahead of the pack, creates demand for products and services. When church and nonprofit leaders develop and introduce fresh insights, they produce growth.

How important is a new perspective? In *The Effective Executive: The Definitive Guide to Getting the Right Things Done*, business analyst Peter F. Drucker tells of a medical supply company knocked from its top position in the industry. The company leaders were shocked because their products were technically superior to those of the rival who outwit them.

GETTING NEW PERSPECTIVES REQUIRES FORCING OURSELVES TO THINK IN NEW WAYS.

Eventually, they learned that their successful competitor didn't win by spending a huge portion of their research budget on technical breakthroughs. Instead of battling them on their own turf, they sent their salesmen into hospitals and doctor's offices, encouraging them to observe and listen to customers, not to sell. The information and fresh insights they gained observing their customers' environment and challenges helped them become the industry's provider of choice.

THE GENESIS OF PERSPECTIVE

Gaining new perspectives is always rewarding, but it requires forcing ourselves to think in new ways. Our tried-and-true methods of thinking won't lead to discovering new methods of competing or fresh paths for serving. Since it's important to be aware of how we develop our thinking, we will examine the six primary origins of perspective:

1. Family
2. Friends
3. Foes
4. Culture
5. Education
6. Ancient wisdom

Our family is the first group that teaches us how to think something through. This is where we get our core values, prejudices, fears, biases, and preferences.

The second origin of our perspective is our friends. They bring all the influences of their families with them. If you have three good friends, all of them will bring their own universes to the table. When you're talking, they'll say, "My mom does this," "My dad says this," "We would never do that," or "Why don't you do that?" Even as kids, they help us think through things because they bring different perspectives.

Then there are our foes, those who don't like us, don't care for us, and don't wish us the very best. When people don't have your best interest in mind, it helps you see things with a different perspective. Perhaps you are in a meeting and you know somebody there wants to undercut you. He is not there for you; he is there to challenge you by raising issues about your department. This is just the way he thinks. The way to win beat the enemy is to think like the enemy. So, you begin to keep your friends close and your enemies closer—because it gives you a new perspective.

KEEP YOUR FRIENDS CLOSE AND YOUR ENEMIES CLOSER.

Our culture also gives us perspective. By culture, I'm talking about regions of the country and parts of the world. If you're from the northeast, and I'm from the south, our cultures are different. We will interact differently, think differently, and perhaps even value things differently.

Our education also shapes our perspective. Because they've been informed at different levels, those with GED or a high school diploma will look at an issue one way, while those with a college education will look at it another way. Both parties have been informed, but at different levels.

Then there's the ancient wisdom that's embedded in our subconscious, which tells us that we should do this but shouldn't do that. The book of Proverbs talks about this. For example, I have been away from my home country India since 1973, yet some of India's ancient wisdom remains a part of me.

OUR ATTITUDES WILL GREATLY INFLUENCE OUR ABILITY TO DEVELOP NEW PERSPECTIVES.

Once we become aware of the boundaries of our thinking, we can proactively push past them to develop new perspectives.

HEALTHY BELIEFS FOSTER NEW PERSPECTIVES

In addition to knowing how we develop perspective, we must be aware of our beliefs, which greatly influence our ability to develop new perspectives.

If we believe that we have to be competent in every area, we will develop an independent spirit. While a certain amount of independence is healthy, we must guard against developing a spirit that will not accept other people's ideas, as this blocks us from gaining new perspectives. We have to be healthy enough and free enough to admit that we cannot be strong in every area.

It's much healthier to focus on developing an interdependent spirit. As leaders, we don't need to know it all; we just need to know people who have strengths that complement ours. We can surround ourselves with people who show us what we need to see, and who help us to understand what we need. I

TRANS-DEPENDENCE KEEPS US ROOTED IN THE PAST, GIVES US CONTEXT FOR THE PRESENT, AND OFFERS US PERSPECTIVE FOR THE FUTURE.

don't need to know how to program a computer; I just need someone who can do it for me. I don't need to see everything; I just need people who can see what I don't see. You must carefully select the right advisors, just as the president carefully chooses his cabinet members. As I mentioned in *Who's Holding Your Ladder?* you have to select the right people to hold your ladder.

HEALTHY LEADERS CAN SAY, "I DON'T KNOW EVERYTHING, I DON'T NEED TO KNOW EVERYTHING, AND THAT'S NOT A SIGN OF WEAKNESS."

In the chapter one, "New People," I mention the three groups of people that we need to be connected with: Those where we were, those where we are, and those where we want to be. I use the term "trans-dependent" to describe how we should relate to these three groups of people. We need all three groups of people in our lives to be healthy. Trans-dependence keeps us rooted in the past, gives us context for the present, and offers us perspective for the future.

Healthy leaders can say, "I don't know everything, I don't need to know everything, and that's not a sign of weakness. I need only to be connected with people who can help me achieve my goals."

Research tells us that leaders with the humility to cultivate a healthy, trans-dependent spirit create winning organizations. In his classic study on the characteristics of great leaders, Jim Collins said that an executive with the odd mix of "extreme personal humility" and "intense professional will" was *the* critical component in all high-performing organizations.[13]

He was shocked by their modesty, by their desire not to talk about themselves but to focus attention on other executives. Collins also found

INSTEAD OF SAYING, "THE BUCK STOPS HERE," GOOD LEADERS SAY, "THE BUCK STARTS HERE."

the inverse to be true: Leaders with huge egos were detrimental to their organizations.[14] While their charisma and skills still lead to beneficial changes, these leaders weren't able to sustain performance at this level.

Being humble as an answer person and being humble as a facilitator of your organization's success are completely different things. Instead of saying, "The buck stops here," good leaders say, "The buck starts here." These leaders get things started, and when they do, they put responsibility into the hands of the right people and *they* stop the buck. They don't know everything, and that's not a bad thing. It's just a different perspective.

13. Jim Collins, "Level 5 Leadership: The Triumph of Humility and Fierce Resolve," *Harvard Business Review*, July-August 2005, https://hbr.org/2005/07/level-5-leadership-the-triumph-of-humility-and-fierce-resolve.
14. Ibid.

CONNECTING PEOPLE AND PERSPECTIVE

Most often, you'll gain new perspective from other people. When you're trying to figure something out, interact with people with other viewpoints to foster new ideas. You'll gain more perspective from other people than you will from attending conferences, reading books, and listening to CDs. When you're searching for new perspective, the place to find it is in other people!

YOU HAVE TO BE COMFORTABLE WITH PEOPLE WHO KNOW MORE THAN YOU.

But to gain this new perspective, you have to be comfortable with people who know more than you. That means that you should beware of always being the smartest person in the room. Continually living in circles in which you're the smartest person is a sad place to be.

WE NEED TO BE AROUND PEOPLE WHO KNOW MORE THAN US SO WE CAN WALK AWAY KNOWING MORE THAN WE DID BEFORE.

There was a time when people would strive to be the smartest one around. Now, more people realize that they need to be around people who are smarter. They realize that the world they're in is not a stationary landscape but a dynamic, ever-changing seascape. There's been a shift in thinking, and more people are saying, "I need to be around people who know more than me, so I can walk away knowing more than I did before."

When you're around smart people, give them sincere permission to speak into your life. You can give consent verbally, but there are other ways of doing it. You can say it through your actions, by attending talks they may be giving or by inviting them to lunch. Once you've given them these signals, they won't hesitate to provide input, and you won't take it as criticism; you'll walk away with a new perspective.

Being open to other people's ideas requires our willingness to put our own ideas aside. It doesn't work if we have a critical spirit that says, "Well, that works for them but not for me." It also won't work when we have a jealous spirit that says, "I should have thought of that!"

We can apply other people's ideas only to the degree we are humble. When you're humble, you won't perceive other people's ideas as threats **WHEN YOU'RE HUMBLE, YOU WILL CALL PEOPLE AND ASK, "WHAT DO YOU THINK?"** but as gifts. When you're humble, you won't just want other people's ideas, you will value and solicit them! When you're humble, you will call people and ask, "What do you think?" Humble leaders know how to solicit other people's ideas. What good is it to ask for someone else's advice and then fight it? If you keep fighting, after a while that person will say, "I'm not going to argue with you. You asked me! And now you want me to give you ten points to corroborate my stance?"

THE MOST IMPORTANT QUESTION THAT ONE HUMAN BEING CAN ASK ANOTHER IS, "WHAT DO YOU THINK?"

The most important question that one human being can ask another is, "What do you think?" No question shows your respect for a person more than that. New perspectives will come when you seek them out. And then you will have intellectual assets—new perspective to apply!

TEN TOOLS FOR YOUR JOURNEY TOWARD NEW PERSPECTIVE

As I close this chapter, I will leave you with ten tools to use on your journey toward new perspective.

1. Ask yourself the "Peter Drucker" questions:

+ What is our mission?

+ Who is our customer?

+ What does our customer value?

+ What is our plan?

+ What are our results?

2. Examine and clarify what you offer. Whatever you offer people is your product. And since this changes over time, thinking about it can change your. What I offered a few years ago—running a college—is not what I offer today, which is life coaching and consultation.

3. *Offer who you are.* What's better: A pastor who gives inspiring sermons or a pastor who gives himself? Certainly, the greatest gift one human being can give another is himself. Giving myself to my wife is very different from working to be a better husband. How do you give yourself to another person? By focusing on who you are, not on what you do. It's all about emphasizing the inner realities over the external realities. In the end, who we are spills over into what we do. (See Proverbs 4:23; Luke 6:45.)

4. *Recertify yourself each year.* Change is always necessary. We cannot assume that just because something works today, it will continue to work tomorrow. You must evolve or you will stagnate.

A leader must continually strive to stay ahead of the game, especially in personal development. Growth and change have been studied for years, but they're occurring at a much faster rate than ever recorded in history.

Most leaders recognize the need for change only after decline has set in; they don't take action until something has broken. This is illustrated by point B on Charles Handy's Sigmoid Curve. At this point, the best they can do is hit the brakes to slow it down, begin some crisis management, and put a spin on it.

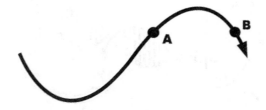

When you're ahead of the curve and making changes (point A), no one may understand what you're doing or why you're doing it. That period between implementing change and others beginning to see what you saw is aptly known as *chaos*. When you begin making changes, people may ask, "Why fix it when it's not broken?" But you can't show them something that they don't have eyes to see.

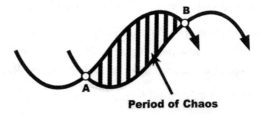

Period of Chaos

Rest assured that there's no way to avoid cycles of chaos. Going from chaos to chaos is how organizations grow, how industries change, and how products evolve. Given that we're always encountering cycles of change, we need to stay ahead of the curve by regularly asking ourselves, "What changes do I need to make?" If we don't, we'll become a part of the landscape. We need to ensure that we're regularly recertifying ourselves, making changes before the need becomes critical.

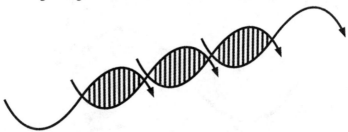

5. *Commit to a personal development plan (PDP).* Many leaders have personal development plans; they just haven't written them down. You should write down new perspectives and chart your progress. Include who you're going to be with and what things you need to bring into your life—conferences you'll attend, periodicals you'll subscribe to, and CDs you'll listen to. Then quarterly check your progress and hold yourself accountable.

6. *Focus on personal disciplines.* Personal disciplines are *the* determining factor in a leader's success. People all over the world ask me, "What do you consider to be *the* make-it-or-break-it issue in leadership?" This is it: personal disciplines. It's not the big stuff that makes or breaks people; it's the small stuff. It's about what time you get up, doing what you say you're going to do, reading books, and being on time. It's about always telling the truth, treating everybody with respect, and returning phone calls and e-mail.

There are many types of personal disciplines you should put into use. First, *respond promptly*. In handling personal contacts, for example, I work by a personal discipline known as

HOW DO YOU RENEW YOURSELF?

OHIO, or "Only Handle It Once." When I get an e-mail or voicemail, I respond right away, so I don't have to deal with it again. Sometimes, I'll forward the message to my assistant to follow up. If I need to respond to an e-mail that will take more time, I reply right away with a short message saying that I got the message and that I will think about the matter and then get back to that person. Then I follow through; it's a matter of personal discipline for me.

Second, *read widely.* I always encourage people to read outside the narrow sphere of their interests, to read about the areas that they want to be in, not the ones they're in right now. I read as much secular literature as I do sacred literature. I read *Fast Company* magazine, the *Leader to Leader* journal, Peter Drucker books, and *Harvard Business Review.* I read all sorts of genres.

"IN TIMES OF CHANGE, LEARNERS INHERIT THE EARTH, WHILE THE LEARNED FIND THEMSELVES BEAUTIFULLY EQUIPPED TO DEAL WITH A WORLD THAT NO LONGER EXISTS."

Third, *grow intentionally.* When Bob Dylan wrote, "He not busy being born is busy dying," he was saying that people need to make sure that they're always renewing themselves. How do you renew yourself? I renew myself by always finding new people to be around, and given my work, that's not a difficult thing to do. I'm always looking for new things to read and for new people who can give me new perspectives, and I have a plan to keep growing.

7. *Remember that the learners outdistance the learned.* Eric Hoffer emphasized the importance of continual learning when

he wrote, "In times of change, learners inherit the earth, while the learned find themselves beautifully equipped to deal with a world that no longer exists." A person with a PhD who has not continued growing is "learned." A person with a GED who continues growing and developing can outdistance that PhD. I may have a graduate degree in computer science, but if I don't keep up with my field, I'm only learned. Unless I'm an active learner, my degree doesn't mean much; it's just looks good on a resume.

8. Be content to be a work in progress. I'm not where I was yesterday, and I'm not where I'm going to be tomorrow. I'm a work in progress. That's a very healthy perspective to have. With this perspective, if you correct me on something today, I won't take umbrage. I will just regard it as part of the growth process.

9. Don't miss out on the joy of the journey. Have you ever heard children on a long trip asking, "Are we there yet?" Their parents patiently encourage them to find ways to enjoy the journey. But what about us? Are *we* enjoying the trip? Are we

> **THERE ARE NO MISTAKES IF WE'VE LEARNED SOMETHING IN THE PROCESS.**

having fun, or are we obsessed with our destination? With the right perspective, we won't let mistakes get us down. We know that we don't have to have it all together; we don't always have to have all the answers because we're a work in progress. There are no mistakes if we've learned something in the process.

10. Ask yourself the following questions at the end of every day:

+ What did I learn today? (What spoke both to my heart and my head?)

+ How did I grow today? (What touched my heart and affected my actions?)

+ What will I do differently tomorrow? (Unless you can tell me what you plan to do differently, you didn't learn anything. There are no mistakes if you've learned something in the process.)

If I were to call you at the end of the day and ask about your day, what would you say? These three questions not only give you something to add to your personal development plan daily, they'll nurture new perspectives and ongoing growth in your life.

Gaining new perspectives is not something that's just going to happen to you; they don't fall out of the sky. You have to make it happen by creating the right conditions and putting yourself in situations that will lead to growth. By regularly working with these tools, you'll put yourself on the right road—the road to new perspectives.

TEACHING POINTS

1. New perspectives are valuable in the business world and provide growth within organizations.

2. Gaining new perspective involves forcing ourselves to think in new ways.

3. To gain new perspective, we should be aware of the six primary origins of perspective: family, friends, foes, culture, education, and ancient wisdom.

    a. Family provides us with our core values, prejudices, fears, biases, and preferences.

    b. Our friends bring us perspectives influenced by their own families.

    c. As we "keep our friends close and our enemies closer," our foes help us develop new perspective.

    d. Our culture also offers us perspective.

    e. Education provides perspective by giving us other ways to think about issues.

    f. Our perspective is also formed by the ancient wisdom embedded in our subconscious.

4. Becoming aware of the borders of our thinking helps us to proactively push past them into new perspectives.

5. Our beliefs greatly influence our ability to develop new perspective.

6. Rather than developing an independent spirit, trying to excel in every area, leaders should be

interdependent, surrounding themselves with people who have complementary strengths.

7. To be healthy, leaders need to be trans-dependent by being connected to those where they were, those where they are, and those where they want to be.

8. Research shows that leaders with a mix of "extreme personal humility" and "intense professional will" are the critical component in all high-performing organizations.

9. Leaders ind new perspective by connecting with other people.

10. Humble leaders value and solicit others' perspectives.

11. Use the following ten tools to help gain new perspective:

    a. Ask yourself the "Peter Drucker" questions:

        i. What is our mission?

        ii. Who is our customer?

        iii. What does our customer value?

        iv. What is our plan?

        v. What are our results?

    b. Regularly evaluate what you offer, as it changes over time.

    c. Offer who you are, not what you do.

d. Avoid crisis by recertifying yourself annually.

e. Commit to a written personal development plan (PDP).

f. Personal disciplines—such as handling personal contacts, reading widely, and growing intentionally—are *the* determining factor in a leader's success.

g. Remember that learners outdistance the learned.

h. Be content to be a work in progress.

i. Don't miss out on the joy of the journey. And remember, there are no mistakes if you've learned something in the process.

j. At the end of every day, focus on what you learned, how you grew, and what you'll do differently tomorrow.

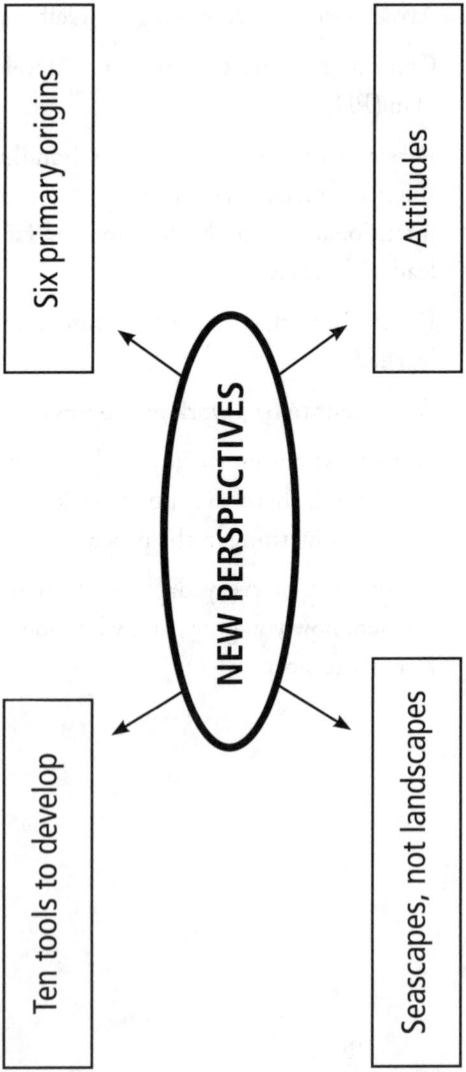

Six primary origins

Attitudes

NEW PERSPECTIVES

Ten tools to develop

Seascapes, not landscapes

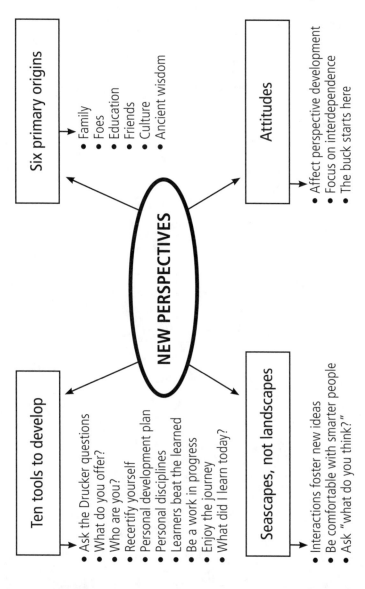

Six primary origins

→
- Family
- Foes
- Education
- Friends
- Culture
- Ancient wisdom

Attitudes

→
- Affect perspective development
- Focus on interdependence
- The buck starts here

NEW PERSPECTIVES

Ten tools to develop

→
- Ask the Drucker questions
- What do you offer?
- Who are you?
- Recertify yourself
- Personal development plan
- Personal disciplines
- Learners beat the learned
- Be a work in progress
- Enjoy the journey
- What did I learn today?

Seascapes, not landscapes

→
- Interactions foster new ideas
- Be comfortable with smarter people
- Ask "what do you think?"

5

NEW PRIORITIES

"There is surely nothing quite so useless as doing with
great efficiency what should not be done at all."[15]
—Peter Drucker

Sitting in his garage workshop, watching the wood shavings
fall from the edge of his knife, Paul felt himself start to relax.
As he did, his thoughts turned to the problems facing his software company.

Despite the company's financial success, Paul instinctively
felt that it was trying to do too many things. After their early
success in creating graphics for computer games, they expanded
and started creating animation sequences for websites and
software programs. They'd even launched their own computer
game, which achieved some industry recognition.

Paul wondered how these activities even related to the
company's vision, which was to be the graphics provider of

---

15. Peter F. Drucker, "Managing for Business Effectiveness," *Harvard Business
Review*, May–June 1963, https://hbr.org/1963/05/managing-for-business-
effectiveness.

choice for the computer-game industry. He'd always assumed that diversifying was beneficial, since it brought in more revenue. Staring at the chisel in his hand, Paul considered how honing his wood-carving tools to a fine edge improved their performance. He wondered what adjustments he could make to gain the same improved performance from his organization.

If you're a Baby Boomer like me, you're probably thinking about downsizing your life. As a generation, we are examining our experiences and getting rid of everything but the essentials. No one wants to be working as hard in his sixties as he did in his forties. But everyone wants to have a bigger impact at sixty than he did at forty. To make that happen, a person must focus his activity; he must hone it to a fine edge.

WHENEVER YOUR ORGANIZATION FOCUSES ON A FEW ESSENTIAL PRIORITIES, IT GAINS STRENGTH.

Leaders at this stage of life hone or focus their efforts in different ways. A pastor might stop pastoring full-time, for example, and use his pastoral-care expertise to consult other pastors. Depending on a person's background, she may become part of a stewardship company and raise money for churches. I limit my focus to one thing—leadership—and I use three delivery systems—consultations; conferences; and resources, including books and CDs. Everything I do involves equipping leaders—that's my priority.

Focusing on priorities is good for organizations, too. Whenever your organization focuses on a few essential priorities, it gains strength. Peter Drucker described organizations as purposefully designed tools created for specialized tasks. The more specialized their task, the greater their strength. On the other hand, "Diversification destroys the performance capacity of an organization,"[16] said Drucker. Organizations are effective only when they're narrowly focused.

Narrowing your priorities gives you momentum and energy. The apostle Paul understood the power of the essential few when he wrote, *"This one thing I do…"* (Philippians 3:13 KJV). His priority was preaching to the Gentiles, just as the apostle Peter's priority was preaching to the Jews.

Most of us are familiar with the power of focusing on a few essential priorities. For example, if I were visiting your town and we decided to go out for a good steak dinner, where would you take me? Chances are that you wouldn't take me to a Shoney's or Denny's or the local diner. When considering where to take me, you would probably think of a steak house, a place that focuses only on cooking steaks. You didn't think of going somewhere that serves breakfast anytime, where you can order liver and onions, spaghetti, and anything else you could want. You intuitively recognized that the better something is, the fewer things it does.

---

16. Peter F. Drucker, "The New Society of Organizations," *Harvard Business Review*, September-October 1992, https://hbr.org/1992/09/the-new-society-of-organizations.

Fulfilling your vision requires you to focus on a few essential priorities. You have to work smarter, not harder. Gaining that critical focus involves answering three important questions:

+ What are my priorities?

+ How should I implement these priorities?

+ How can I effectively communicate my priorities within my organization?

FINDING THE ESSENTIAL FEW

To define your priorities, start by examining your vision. Your vision and your priorities will always be inextricably linked. That's because your vision is the source of your priorities. It provides you with the necessary context and helps you define your priorities.

YOUR VISION IS THE SOURCE OF YOUR PRIORITIES.

For example, my own vision is empowering leaders. My website explains that my vision is creating a leadership culture, helping others to succeed, and developing leaders who produce other leaders. That vision provides a context for what my priorities should be and should not be. For example, my priorities should not be focused on praise and worship, theology, or church growth. They should involve leadership.

Now, that doesn't mean that I won't have influence in those other areas. There will always be some overlap, but my primary focus is leadership.

When your vision provides the context for your priorities, you will find that it is much easier to make decisions. For example, let's say that I have two speaking opportunities but both opportunities are on the same day. I have to decide whether I will preach to a crowd of 10,000 people or a crowd of 100 leaders. I don't even have to think about it; my mind is already made up. Because my vision provides me with context, you'll find me in a room with the 100 leaders.

However, don't make the mistake of thinking that once you've established your priorities, they're forever carved in stone. Peter Drucker said, "Every product and every activity begins to obsolesce as soon as it is started.[17] We can

EVERY PRODUCT, DECISION, AND BUSINESS ACTIVITY IS HEADED FOR OBSOLESCENCE THE MINUTE IT BEGINS.

blame it on market shifts, cultural pressures, or even the third law of thermodynamics, but it's inevitable.

Effective leaders are constantly reevaluating their priorities, regularly checking to ensure that they're focused on the right activities. As mentioned in the chapter 4, "New Perspectives," we cannot assume that just because something works today, it will continue to work tomorrow. It's important to ensure that what was important yesterday is still important today. Don't wait for situations to decline before you evaluate your priorities;

---

17. Drucker, "Managing for Business Effectiveness."

stay ahead of the game by remaining aware of the environment and continually evaluating your priorities.

MAKE THE MOST OF YOUR TIME BY SCHEDULING YOUR PRIORITIES RATHER THAN PRIORITIZING YOUR SCHEDULE.

Obviously, your priorities should affect how you invest your time. It's important that you make the most of your time by *scheduling your priorities* rather than *prioritizing your schedule.* When you prioritize your schedule, you simply look at your priorities and rank what's most important; but when you schedule your priorities, you proactively allocate time to each priority. This ensures that you devote time to what's most important to you, and it will help you to achieve your vision.

PUTTING YOUR PRIORITIES TO WORK

Once you determine your priorities, it's important to develop a strategic plan to implement them. This will help ensure that your priorities mesh with your organization's vision. For example, if you were developing priorities for the Ritz-Carlton Hotel Company, you would ensure that each priority reflected the hotel's vision of providing stellar customer service to all guests.

Developing a strategic plan to implement your priorities involves answering a number of questions:

+ How does this priority support our vision?

+ In what specific ways can we implement this priority?

+ Who will be responsible for these activities?

+ What's the time frame for accomplishing this priority?

+ Do we have the resources, such as the finances, people, and facilities, to undertake this right now? How will we measure success?

Your answers to these questions will ensure that your vision, mission, values, and priorities all are properly aligned. In my book *What's Shaking Your Ladder?* I call this alignment "organizational congruence," which provides focus, energy, and passion. You know where you're going, where you're *not* going, how you'll get there, and when you arrive.

Whenever you implement new priorities, you will have to deal with a variety of obstacles. It would be great if you could instantly adopt, plan, and execute new priorities, but that rarely happens. Organizations are made up of people, and people do not handle instant change well. They need time to transition, so you will have to help them make the necessary emotional, psychological, and relational adaptations.

ORGANIZATIONAL CONGRUENCE PROVIDES FOCUS, ENERGY, AND PASSION.

It's not always wise or possible to completely disengage from old priorities when new ones emerge. If your new priority involved providing a new service or entering a new market, you might not want to—or be able to—stop offering your other products or disengage from other markets. Your staff may have emotional ties with products and services to which they've grown accustomed. They may also have reservations about competing in a new market. For these and many other reasons, it's best to plan for transitions.

When I was preparing to resign as president of Beulah Heights Bible College, I spent a lot of time planning for the transition. I met with the board members individually and explained what I was going to do and why; consulted with highly influential leaders who had made significant transitions themselves; and developed a successor. The point is this: I couldn't immediately disengage from old priorities; I had to prepare a transition plan. I had to disengage from old priorities without completely discarding them, while also moving forward with my new priorities.

Another common challenge in implementing priorities is protecting yourself from well-intentioned people who want to impose their priorities on you. People always have helpful suggestions, so you must be sold on your priorities and unwavering in your decision to see them through. This resolve will help you diplomatically deal with distractions.

Rick Warren says that he's always meeting people who suggest that Saddleback Church adopt practices from their last church. They tell him, "At our old church, we did it like this…." He says he finds himself wondering how he can politely inform them that Saddleback has its own vision. Rick Warren understands the importance of staying true to his God-given vision and priorities.

Now that's not to say that people won't provide valuable suggestions and that you shouldn't consider them, and you don't want to discourage input. You just have to ensure that their suggestions fit with your vision, don't overextend your resources, and are not imposed on you. Your priorities must be birthed by your vision.

YOUR PRIORITIES MUST BE BIRTHED BY YOUR VISION.

When you know your destiny, your purpose, and your God-given priorities, you know what you're built to do, which makes it easier to stay focused and keep other people—however well-intentioned—from choosing or changing your priorities.

COMMUNICATING PRIORITIES TO OTHERS

If you want people to get behind the organization's priorities and make them their own, you first have to sell them on your vision. Noted expert on organizational change and transition William Bridges said that people won't understand the solution you propose (your vision and priorities) until they understand the problem. It's a leader's job to explain what needs to happen and why.

PEOPLE WILL NOT UNDERSTAND THE SOLUTION UNTIL THEY UNDERSTAND THE PROBLEM.

Getting people engaged with your vision and priorities involves more than making an announcement or holding a meeting or two to discuss them. You have to communicate persuasively; you have to sell them your vision just as you would sell it to investors. You have to cast your vision just as you would cast a line to catch a fish.

Getting people engaged with a vision and priorities is known as the art of vision casting.

To effectively cast your vision,

+ *Keep it simple.* Articulate your vision and priorities in terms that people understand. Keep it as simple as possible. The simpler, the better. Use short sentences and short words. You're really aiming at making it digestible.

+ *Make it memorable.* Make the vision easy to remember. My vision, for example, is helping others succeed. Your vision should be short enough to fit on a T-shirt. If it doesn't, people won't remember it.

+ *Maintain a stable vision.* Over time, your vision and priorities will expand, but their essence shouldn't change. If you continually change your vision, your supporters will get confused.

+ *Be patient.* Most important, when you establish new priorities, give people time to catch on. Remember that by the time we unveil new priorities to our organization, we've been living with them for quite some time. We've had time to engage with them, and they've become a part of us. Too many leaders make the mistake of thinking that people should jump aboard our vision after a few staff meetings. It doesn't work that quickly. Your people are just beginning their own journey with these new priorities. Be patient with them and always find ways to help them acclimate to change.

An example of an organization that's realizing the benefit of people engaged with its vision and priorities is the Web retailer Amazon. Their vision is focused on creating the world's most customer-centered company, where people can find and buy anything online.

According to CEO Jeff Bezos, one of Amazon's priorities is conserving money for things that matter.[18] All employee desks—even those of the executives—are modeled after the one Bezos built for himself from a door, a few metal brackets, and two-by-fours when he started the company. That's one creative way to communicate a priority!

Some of Amazon's business decisions seem risky. If you've ever visited the website, you know that people often post online reviews of their products. In some cases, the reviews are pretty negative. Bezos says that when they started allowing customers to write review, people told him he didn't understand much about business. In his mind, however, enabling people to post online reviews was fulfilling Amazon's vision because it assisted customers in making purchasing decisions.

18. Alan Deutschman, "Inside the Mind of Jeff Bezos," *Fast Company*, August 1, 2004, http://www.fastcompany.com/50541/inside-mind-jeff-bezos.

Did you know that Amazon even warns customers when they're about to purchase a product they previously purchased from the site? This might seem like another example of poor business sense to many companies; but it perfectly aligns with Amazon's customer-centered vision.

Like Amazon, you can find strength by focusing your energy on only a few essential priorities.

TEACHING POINTS

1. Fewer priorities lead to bigger impact.

2. A focused organization is strong, while diversifying destroys its capacity to perform.

3. The better we are, the fewer things we do.

4. To establish focus, we should ask ourselves, "What are our priorities?" "How should we implement them?" and "How can we effectively communicate them within our organization?"

5. To discover our priorities, we should examine our vision, which is the source and context of our priorities.

6. Knowing our priorities simplifies decision-making.

7. We should regularly reevaluate our priorities to ensure proper focus rather than wait for situations to decline.

8. We should schedule our priorities instead of prioritizing our schedule, devoting time to what's most important.

9. We can develop a strategic plan by asking ourselves:

    a. How does this priority support our vision?

    b. In what specific ways can we implement this priority?

    c. Who will be responsible for these activities?

    d. What's the time frame for accomplishing this priority?

    e. Do we have the necessary resources, such as the finances, people, and facilities, to undertake this right now? How will we measure success?

10. Organizational congruence is achieved when our vision, values, and priorities are aligned.

11. We must help people in your organization to make the necessary emotional, psychological, and relational adaptations that are part of the transition to new priorities.

12. It's not always wise or possible to completely disengage from old priorities when new ones emerge. Instead, we must plan for transitions.

13. We must guard against others who impose their priorities on us.

14. People will not understand the solution until they understand the problem.

15. When communicating priorities, remember that we must sell our vision.

16. When casting our vision, we should keep it simple, memorable, and stable. And be patient.

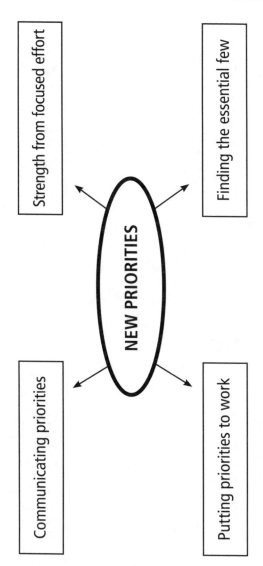

Strength from focused effort

Finding the essential few

NEW PRIORITIES

Communicating priorities

Putting priorities to work

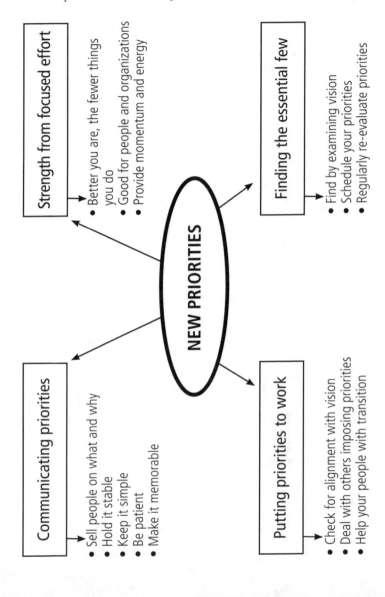

Strength from focused effort

→
- Better you are, the fewer things you do
- Good for people and organizations
- Provide momentum and energy

Finding the essential few

→
- Find by examining vision
- Schedule your priorities
- Regularly re-evaluate priorities

NEW PRIORITIES

Communicating priorities

→
- Sell people on what and why
- Hold it stable
- Keep it simple
- Be patient
- Make it memorable

Putting priorities to work

→
- Check for alignment with vision
- Deal with others imposing priorities
- Help your people with transition

6

NEW PASSIONS

"There is a time for everything, and a season for every activity under the heavens."
—Ecclesiastes 3:1

Jake wasn't really sick; he just couldn't face another day of lengthy meetings, phone calls, and planning sessions. Driving to the golf course, he began feeling guilty, thinking that he was behaving more like a student cutting class than senior pastor of a growing church.

If this was the only day he'd played hooky, he might have felt differently. But Jake's increased need for unscheduled time off, lengthy periods of daydreaming, and loss of focus were beginning to concern him. Despite a two-week vacation, he was still just as edgy and restless. Was it burnout or a midlife crisis?

Jake pulled his golf clubs out from the trunk of the car, set them on the concrete, and stared at the clubhouse with his hands in his pockets. He'd always thought that counseling was for weaker souls without goals or purpose. Was he wrong?

Lost in his thoughts, he didn't notice or hear the valet until he tugged gently on Jake's sleeve.

It might be hard for you to imagine this now, especially if you're in the early stages of realizing your vision, but, as your journey continues, you may discover that the dreams and visions that once compelled you begin to lose their luster. In fact, they might someday become routine, even boring.

You might shake your head at the thought. You cannot imagine yourself feeling less fulfilled let alone feeling bored by what you're doing. But it happens. And when it does, it's important that you remember that it's entirely natural.

Or maybe you're experiencing this shift right now, saying, "Yes, that's me."

IT'S TYPICAL FOR VISIONARY LEADERS TO BECOME UNCOMFORTABLE WITH THE STATUS QUO.

When my own vision began to lose its luster, I wasn't quite sure why. I responded by making myself busier, diving into my duties as president of Beulah Heights Bible College with renewed commitment. However, as hard as I tried, the boredom, the feelings that I had done all this before, and the sense that there were no new mountains to climb did not go away. I thought that there was something wrong with me. It took me a while to learn that what I was experiencing was quite normal.

No leader—not even Bill Gates—is exempt from these changes in passion. When Gates started Microsoft, his passion about his work was evident whenever he spoke. Talk with him today, though, and you might be surprised to find that his passion has shifted. That's exactly what one journalist for *New York* magazine discovered while listening to Gates speak shortly after he stepped down as CEO of Microsoft to run the Gates Foundation:

> It was clear to all in the auditorium that software no longer got Gates's juices pumping the way his work at the foundation did. Technology questions were answered quickly, without passion, whereas questions about global health elicited lengthy disquisitions full of detail and emotion. The way he talked about wiping out malaria was how he used to talk about wiping out Netscape.[19]

Now that's a change in passion!

It's typical for visionary leaders to become uncomfortable with the status quo. They are often exemplary leaders when it comes to reviving a dying company or launching a brand-new effort; but they are not equipped to run its daily operations for an extended period. Put a gifted visionary in an operating

---

19. John Heilemann, "The Softening of a Software Man," *New York*, January 9, 2006, http://nymag.com/nymetro/news/columns/powergrid/15456/index1.html.

environment for too long, and he becomes restless and bored, ready for another challenge.

PUT A GIFTED VISIONARY IN AN OPERATING ENVIRONMENT FOR TOO LONG, AND HE BECOMES RESTLESS AND BORED, READY FOR ANOTHER CHALLENGE.

Peter Cuneo, vice chairman and former president and CEO of Marvel Entertainment, described the limits of this talent quite well: "We turnaround types are often the wrong person to lead a well-oiled machine. Typically I stay for three or four years and then move on."[20] No wonder Cuneo is well-known for performing successful turnarounds at seven consumer-product companies, including Clairol, Black & Decker, Remington, and Marvel. He's aware of his gift and listens to the inner voice of his own passion.

Remember, there's nothing wrong with a visionary leader who doesn't get excited when he's gone as far as his gift permits, who wants to move on once the company is performing well. The trick is to know when it's happening to you. As the song says, "You've got to know when to hold 'em, know when to fold 'em."[21]

---

20. Julia Hanna, "Mr. Superhero," *HBS Alumni Bulletin*, vol. 81, no. 4, December 2005, http://hbswk.hbs.edu/archive/5149.html.
21. Kenny Rogers, "The Gambler," 1978.

NAVIGATING CHANGING PASSIONS

Legends of Alexander the Great say that when he realized that he had conquered the entire known world, he sat down and cried because there were no more mountains for him to climb. Maybe that's what you're feeling.

As I described in my book *Who Moved Your Ladder?* when president of Beulah Heights Bible College, I awoke early one morning, thought of my schedule for the day, and wanted to call in sick. I'd worked very hard to make the college successful, and events filled my calendar every day, but there I was, fighting boredom and restlessness. It was a difficult time.

During the months I spent navigating my changing passions, I learned some truths that might help you on your own journey. Navigating changing passions is easier when you can...

+ Admit when things have changed.

+ Act on godly discontent.

+ Leave on a high note.

Admit when things have changed. This sounds too simple to even state. However, visionaries have to learn to slow down and listen to themselves. That isn't always easy for us. Navigating my changing passions began when I could admit that I was having a problem. It wasn't the school that was the problem; the problem was

VISIONARIES HAVE TO LEARN TO SLOW DOWN AND LISTEN TO THEMSELVES.

me, Sam Chand! I had to admit that I was drifting, that I was bored, that the things that used to excite me didn't do so anymore. My life had become a routine, something I felt I could do in my sleep.

Many leaders have a hard time admitting such things, especially if they're visionaries. They don't want to see themselves just going through the motions or standing still. We tell ourselves that we're tired, burned out, or that we need to get away and recharge our batteries. We always want to be going somewhere, so we fill up our schedules, getting busier and busier. But activity isn't always progress.

ACTIVITY ISN'T ALWAYS PROGRESS. Take time to analyze what's going on inside you; continued neglect of your feelings can have negative repercussions. It can drive you into a funk or a depression, which will affect your decision-making as well as your relationships.

Act on godly discontent. It's easy to identify something that's *not* godly discontent. For example, some leaders move to avoid dealing with problems. They act out of human nature, not godly discontent. This is why I always advise leaders to avoid making any high-level transitions before checking the health of their organization. Leaders should always make sure that they're not avoiding working through some difficult issues.

Others assume that their feelings of restlessness arise from their reaching the level of their incompetence. They've hit a wall, and think they can no longer do an adequate job. Moving on isn't the answer, though, because they would only be avoiding dealing with issues of their own personal growth. If they lack competency in a certain area, such as the ability to relate to certain types of people, it will follow them wherever they go. They must work through it.

A leader who acts on godly discontent wants the best for himself and his organization. If he decides to move on, no one will be shortchanged. If he stays, it will create growth for him and his organization. Godly discontent pushes leaders to work through today's challenges so they are prepared for new ones.

Leave on a high note. When I left the college, I could say that I met each goal and challenge that confronted me. I left on a high note by communicating my intent to the board, preparing a successor to ensure the continued success of the organization, and maintaining a positive attitude.

There's nothing to gain by burning your bridges when you go. You never know when you'll need something from your former organization. Don't use your final days to vent your anger or dissatisfaction. Resolve issues before you depart, and leave with a smile on your face. Choosing to move on is always a difficult decision, but venting negative feelings just makes it more difficult for everyone.

Regardless of how challenging it might be, stay focused on the positive. While I'm an optimistic person, I found more faults in my last few months at the college than in all previous fourteen years combined. And I had to ask myself why this was happening. I concluded that it was because I subconsciously needed to convince myself I was making the right decision. I kept telling myself that I wasn't leaving because something was wrong but because I was ready for the next step in my own life.

UNCOVERING NEW PASSIONS

There are a lot books written to help people cope with being fired or laid off. But there's not much to tell you how to cope with transitions when you're doing well, when you're successful, when you've achieved more than you've ever dreamed. When I searched for resources to assist me through my transition, I found little that helped me deal with my decision and issues.

WHAT DO YOU DO WHEN ONE IS PASSION IS INCREASING AND ANOTHER IS DECREASING?

So what do you do when one passion is increasing and another is decreasing? These times of transition are not comfortable. Years ago, *Fast Company* profiled businessmen who were transitioning between long-term corporate jobs and running their own businesses, and found that "corporate dropouts concede that one of the most difficult things [during transition] is to maintain the same level of enthusiasm for the job you're about to leave as the venture you're about to start."[22] In my case, my passion for con-

---

22. Michael A. Prospero, "Exit Strategies for Corporate Dropouts," *Fast Company*, April 1, 2005, http://www.fastcompany.com/55401/exit-strategies-corporate-dropouts.

sulting was increasing while my passion for leading the college was decreasing. This disturbed my equilibrium. But during this time of transition, I kept both irons in the fire, because I had made peace with where my passions were.

Uncovering a new passion is also challenging. Some leaders find their passion in less-than-ideal circumstances. When Steve Case retired shortly after the AOL-Time Werner merger, he followed his passion by launching a company that focused on providing consumer-friendly health-care services, inspired partly by his brother's brain-cancer diagnosis and partly by his own frustrations with finding a doctor for a sick child on the weekend.

Discerning your own passion may not happen quickly. You may have to seek it out, which requires a great deal of soul-searching, trusting your instincts, and asking yourself many hard questions. To discern your passion, consider your core values and dreams. Ask yourself...

+ What do I really care about?

+ What makes me pound the table with passion?

+ What do I dream about?

+ Where do I get my greatest fulfillment?

+ What values are at work in my daydreams?

+ What have I liked most about my work?

Many leaders find this uncomfortable at first, because they are used to dealing with tangible, clear results, while these deliberations can be evasive and hard to measure. But keep with it.

Once you think you've found your passion, ask if you're passionate enough to stay at it for the rest of your professional career. If your passion is fickle or temporary, consider your motives for moving in that direction. If you think your passion will stand the test of time, that's a good indication that you're headed down the right path.

Furthermore, we need to stay on course, which requires getting some help. People don't realize their passions for many reasons. Sometimes, they lack a clearly defined goal and have no way of keeping themselves motivated. Other times, they do not devote enough time to their passion.

You may not have a clear picture of your passion, but you can make it clearer by doing the short exercise on the next page. Once you take one step, you can then commit to taking another small step, and so on. And make sure you find someone who will keep you accountable to in realizing your dream. We need others' support. Then you will take the many small steps needed to realize that big dream. Once I knew where I had to go, where my passion was leading me, I became alive again. And I believe that, if you've lost your passion, once you find yourself headed in the right direction, your own passion will return.

> "The jump is so frightening between where I am and where I could be... [but] because of all I may become, I will close my eyes and leap!"[23]
>
> —Mary Anne Radmacher

---

23. Used by permission.

STEPS TO UNCOVERING YOUR PASSION

1. Write down a short description of your dream.

_____

_____

_____

_____

_____

2. Write down the first step you will take to fulfill your dream.

_____

_____

_____

_____

_____

3. Write down a date on which will have completed the first step.

_____

_____

_____

_____

_____

4.   Next, give someone a copy of this sheet and ask him or her to contact you on that date to see if you've taken the first step.

_____

_____

_____

_____

_____

5.   If you complete the first step, fill out another copy of the sheet, and commit to the next small step.

_____

_____

_____

_____

_____

6.   If you do not complete the first step, change the date and try again!

_____

_____

_____

_____

_____

TEACHING POINTS

1. Our passions shift at various stages of life. It's perfectly normal for something that was once a passionate pursuit to become a mere interest.

2. No leader is exempt from changes in passion.

3. Put a gifted visionary in an operating environment for too long, and he becomes restless and bored, ready for another challenge.

4. There's nothing wrong with a visionary leader who no longer gets excited and wants to move on once a company is performing well.

5. Navigating changing passions is easier when we can admit things have changed, act on godly discontent, and leave on a high note.

6. Many leaders have a hard time admitting they have a problem. They need to take some time and pay attention to their feelings.

7. Leaders look for godly discontent that prepares them for new challenges. This godly discontent is shown in their wanting the best for themselves and their organization.

8. We can leave on a high note by remembering that you're leaving to take the next step in your life.

9. There's little guidance for leaders in times of transition, who feel lost when they've achieved more than they've ever dreamed.

10. Uncovering a new passion is challenging. It requires a great deal of soul-searching, trusting our instincts, and asking ourselves many hard questions.

11. Uncovering our passion involves finding our path and staying on course.

    a. Finding our path involves thinking about our core values and dreams.

    b. If we think we can stay at what we're considering for the rest of our professional career, we may be headed down the right path.

12. People don't realize their passions because they lack a clearly defined goal, they have no way of keeping themselves motivated, and they do not devote time to their passion.

13. Staying on course and realizing our dream involve getting someone else to keep us accountable. Once we take one step, we can then commit to taking another small step, and so on, until we realize our dreams.

14. Once we find ourselves headed in the right direction, our passion will return.

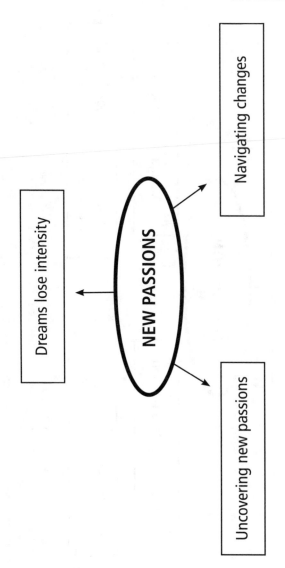

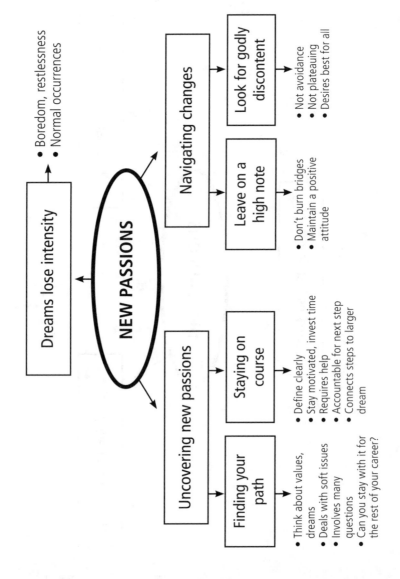

7

NEW PREPARATION

"Forewarned, forearmed;
to be prepared is half the victory."
—Miguel de Cervantes

Disturbed by a conversation he couldn't get out of his head, Pastor Jake Barrett was making little progress on his sermon. Earlier that day, he called a friend pastoring in another state, only to find the man wrestling with concerns over the upcoming closing of a nearby military base, an event that would cause more than half the families in the church to relocate. Jake had listened as the shocked pastor talked about how loss would affect the church's building program, its Christian school, and about his concern for the church's future.

Browsing through his membership roster, Jake wondered what effect this would have on his own congregation. How prepared would they be if one or more of the area's largest employers decided to consolidate facilities elsewhere? What about more immediate concerns? Was he preparing church members to replace deacons and Sunday-school teachers who might leave the area upon retirement? Looking at the calendar on his desk, he wondered how he could possibly equip himself and others to deal with whatever tomorrow might bring.

We control very little in our lives. For leaders who value planning, this can be especially trying. Not long ago, someone could develop a strategic plan, create the associated processes, and be fairly confident of the outcome. Now, due to an accelerated rate of change, we must do more than plan; we must prepare.

WE MUST DO MORE THAN PLAN; WE MUST PREPARE.

Many leaders don't understand the difference between planning and preparation. They make the mistake of thinking of them as synonymous, when they're not. Planning has a narrow focus, while preparation has a much broader focus. When you *plan*, you devise a method to achieve some specific end. When you *prepare*, you ready yourself in advance, you prime yourself, or get warmed up for any possibility. For example, if you feel led into ministry, you will probably prepare yourself by attending Bible school or seminary. You would take Greek and Hebrew classes and study the New and Old Testaments to ready yourself for what you would do.

Let's say that you thought about becoming a pastor, but you really aren't sure. One day, you hear a presentation about the work being done by a specific organization. You realize immediately that this is what you are called to do; it fits you in so many ways. Now that you know what you want to do—work with that organization—you begin planning by taking certain courses and investigating what that organization looks for in potential employees.

There is certainly a time for planning, but we cannot overlook the importance of preparation. Proverbs reminds us, *"The mind of man plans his way, but the LORD directs his steps"* (Proverbs 16:9 NASB). In the end, we have to be ready to follow God's lead, even if that means going somewhere that isn't in our original plans. We simply have to be prepared for whatever comes our way.

Our work environment, business competition, and the entire world are changing rapidly. We cannot assume that today's conditions will remain true tomorrow. All too quickly, the land we're standing on becomes

I KNOW TOO MANY ORGANIZATIONS WHOSE LANDSCAPES HAVE CHANGED, BUT THEY STILL FOLLOW THE SAME STRATEGIC PLAN.

a raging sea. If we're going to successfully surf that sea, we have to be prepared.

I know too many organizations whose landscapes have changed, but they still follow the same strategic plan. That's the result of inadequate preparation on many levels. Rather than articulate our strategic plans with a landscape perspective, we must adopt both the outlook and the language of the sea.

LEADER PREPARATION

How can we prepare for what lies ahead, for the inevitable changes we'll confront? And how can we best prepare the organizations we serve?

As leaders, we must be prepared in several areas. Just as a doctor conducts routine physicals, we must regularly check our preparedness in the following areas:

Personal Preparation

We have to examine how our characters and hang-ups might affect future endeavors. For example, if you're in sales, you'll never excel until you're adept in the art of chitchat. You have to be comfortable with small talk. "Hey, how are you?" "Tell me about your family."" A person who gets right to the point to sell his widget won't be as effective as someone who can establish rapport. Regardless of your field, you have to spend time thinking about what character-related adjustments can help prepare you for the future. I will discuss this important area of preparation in more detail below.

Professional Preparation

THERE IS SIMPLY NO SUBSTITUTE FOR PROFESSIONAL PREPAREDNESS.

We also have to be prepared in our area of professional competency. We have to stay ahead of the curve. If you work with computers, for example, you'll want to be informed of the latest hardware and software. If you're a tax accountant, you'll want to be familiar with the upcoming and most recent changes in laws. We also should pursue whatever certifications we might need in our field. There is simply no substitute for professional preparedness.

Relational Preparation

It's important to be aware of our chemistry with others, or how we get along with people. How comfortable are we meeting new people? Are there certain types of people whom we find difficult to work with? How well do we manage and negotiate conflict? In the end, if we don't relationally click with someone, we may find ourselves limited. That's why it's important to be relationally prepared.

Familial Preparation

We simply cannot ignore the importance of preparing our family. Sometimes, this can be fairly simple. For example, preparing my children for my job change required a simple explanation of the work I was going to do when I left my role at the college. I didn't want them wondering what their dad did. Other times, the preparation might be more complex, such as when we have to relocate. We have to prepare our family members for the new priorities and pains they'll face in a new place.

WE SIMPLY CANNOT IGNORE THE IMPORTANCE OF PREPARING OUR FAMILY.

Financial Preparation

When president of the college, I was paid very well. So when I started my own leadership consulting business, I had to be ready for no regular paycheck, no benefits, and no paid vacation. My wife and I prepared by talking about how to organize our finances. We asked ourselves what expenses we could downsize. If you're considering changes in your organization, you may have to make similar changes in your budget. Even if you don't have the information you need for detailed planning, you can make financial preparations for what might be coming.

Educational Preparation

Many people work in areas in which they have no formal education. It's rare that you find someone working in the same discipline they studied in college. I don't have any formal training in leadership consulting, so I have had to constantly educate myself through the many avenues available to me, such as attending seminars, subscribing to magazines, and reading books. I have to make sure that I'm preparing myself educationally for what lies ahead. In some ways, I feel like a trailblazing pioneer.

THE PERSONAL PREPAREDNESS OF CHARACTER

When preparing, we simply cannot neglect our characters. They may seem inconsequential to helping us reach our destiny, but if we prepare them, too, we will find that our chances of fulfilling your destiny are greatly increased! Each of the following steps are necessary; there are no shortcuts in preparing our character. In the order given, we must take control of our...

1. Thoughts

2. Words

3. Decisions

4. Actions

5. Habits

6. Character

7. Destiny

1. Thoughts

Every man-made thing that you see in the world began as a thought. Your light fixtures, your car, the chair you're sitting on, the book you're reading—they all began as thoughts. We must be careful what we dwell on. If we allow negative thinking to fill our minds, we will not walk in into our destinies! When the Bible says, "[As a man] *thinks in his heart, so is he*" (Proverbs 23:7 NKJV), it's telling us that our thoughts shape who we are; they shape our destiny. Everything begins with a thought, and these thoughts are expressed through our words.

2. Words

Typically, we verbalize our thoughts about our destiny, saying things like, "I wonder what it would be like if...." It's easy to imagine Wilbur and Orville Wright saying, "I wonder what it would be like if we could fly," or Henry Ford saying, "I wonder what it would be like if we could mass-produce cars," or Thomas Edison saying, "I wonder what it would be if we could bring light to the modern home." The book of Genesis tells us that our words our powerful. It was the Word of God that created what we now see around us. Everything began as a thought in God's mind, which led to His saying, *"Let Us make man in Our image"* (Genesis 1:26 NKJV). As with our thoughts, we must control our words.

3. Decisions

Spoken words lead to decisions. You might tell someone, "This is what I'm going to do." We should decide to do things that will help us fulfill our destiny, not cripple it. And decisions lead to actions.

4. Actions

People tend to believe that they can start their journey by first taking action. For example, if they want to lose twenty pounds, they immediately start doing something about it. Unfortunately, jumping into behavior modification is not the appropriate starting place. Statistics show that 80 percent of people who lose weight gain it all back. Decisions without prior thoughts, words, and decisions do not have strong foundations for success.

For example, successful weight loss begins in your thoughts. It may involve considering how being overweight has affected you. Then you might start telling yourself, your family, and your friends, "I need to lose weight. I think I'm going to go on a diet and start exercising." Then you make decisions about what practical changes you're going to make, such as the foods you are going to eat and the exercises you're going to do. There's nothing wrong with taking action, but if you want to be successful, you cannot ignore importance of your thoughts, words, and decisions.

5. Habits

When you continue the same action long enough, it becomes a habit. We all know people who are habitually late. It's not an occasional occurrence; they do it all the time. It comes from lazy thinking and talking, and a lack of good decisions and subsequent actions. All these foundational behaviors are important because they create habits. And it's our habits that create our character.

6. Character

Our character is the sum of our habits. When Aristotle wrote, "We are what we repeatedly do," he made it clear that there's a direct connection between who we are and what we do. He underscored this by concluding, "Excellence, then, is not an act, but a habit." A habit that's performed long enough becomes a part of your character. If you know people who are habitually late, you know that it's hard to expect different behavior from them. Their habit has become part of who they are; it has shaped their character.

7. Destiny

Eventually, your character will lead you into your destiny. There are no shortcuts to success, no easy roads to get there.

Everybody wants to have his or her destiny fulfilled, but not everyone wants to take all the steps to get there.

Realizing your destiny requires deliberate thought and action. You have to continually guard and train your thoughts, because whatever you dwell on is what you'll bring about. (See Proverbs 4:23; 2 Corinthians 10:5.) You must first be prepared before you can reach your destiny. Everything you think, say, and do must be congruent with it. If it isn't, you won't be prepared to go where you want to go!

THE REWARDS OF PREPARATION

Let's face it, despite our research, strategies, and plans, many unplanned things can happen. While we may not be able to control these events, we can control how prepared we are. Prepared leaders can make a world of difference.

OPPORTUNITIES COME TO THOSE WHO ARE PREPARED.

Opportunities come to those who are prepared. When we're prepared, we recognize the right opportunities when they come our way. When we're unprepared, we don't see or grasp these opportunities. As someone once said, "Opportunities are never postponed; they are lost forever." And Leonard Ravenhill once said, "The opportunity of a lifetime must be seized within the lifetime of the opportunity."

Being prepared also provides confidence. It's like the Chinese proverb "When the student is ready, the teacher will appear." When you're prepared, you'll be ready for the right opportunity. The danger in lack of preparation is that we...

> **"THE OPPORTUNITY OF A LIFETIME MUST BE SEIZED WITHIN THE LIFETIME OF THE OPPORTUNITY."**

+ Are blind to obvious opportunities.

+ Cannot mobilize quickly enough to take advantage of new opportunities.

+ Do not attract the right partners.

On the other hand, being prepared will pave the way to success, which is simply the intersection of preparation and opportunity.

> **SUCCESS IS SIMPLY THE INTERSECTION OF OUR PREPARATION AND OUR OPPORTUNITY.**

There's no better example of the benefits of preparation than the Lewis and Clark expedition. Here were leaders facing unknown challenges, about to travel into a wild and hostile environment, who could not know what was around the riverbend.

Their maps were extremely limited. Meriwether Lewis, who had planned the expedition, had little information beyond the

Ohio valley. To make matters worse, they couldn't send scouts beyond the Mississippi to gather information because of hostile French and Spanish armies. They couldn't plan, because too much was out of their control; but they had to be prepared for Indian attacks, for running out of supplies, and for other hardships.

How did they transform what sounded like a suicide mission into a successful expedition, one that's still taught and celebrated two hundred years later? Their success was credited to Lewis' preparation: "It was his meticulous preparations, not a grand sense of adventure, that ultimately ensured the expedition accomplished everything it had been tasked to do and more."[24] We can learn much from the leadership example of Lewis and Clark. Our journey may not be as historic, but our environment sometimes appears just as wild, doesn't it?

Can we afford to be any less prepared? How are we preparing ourselves for tomorrow as we take steps to fulfill our destiny?

TEACHING POINTS

1. Today, planning is difficult because of the accelerated rate of change. That's why we must be prepared.

2. Planning involves devising methods to achieve a specific result. Preparation is broader in scope, and involves readying and priming ourselves for any possibility.

---

24. Lt. Col. Mark J. Reardon, "With Resolute and Thorough Planning: Captain Meriwether Lewis's Preparations for the Journey to the Pacific Ocean," US Army Center of Military History, http://www.history.army.mil/lc/The%20Mission/planning_and_preparation.htm.

3. We cannot assume that today's conditions will remain true tomorrow. We must be prepared for whatever comes our way.

4. As leaders, we must pursue several types of preparation, including...

   a. *Personal preparation* involves examining how our character and hang-ups might affect future endeavors.

   b. *Professional preparation* involves remaining current in the area of our professional competency.

   c. *Relational preparation* involves being aware of our chemistry and our ability to get along with all types of people.

   d. *Familial preparation* involves preparing those we love for whatever they will face.

   e. *Financial preparation* involves organizing our income and expenses for the future.

   f. *Educational preparation* involves remaining current in your area of expertise, which may require reading, joining professional associations, and attending seminars.

5. Prepared leaders recognize new opportunities that come their way.

6. Preparation guards us against becoming opportunistic.

7. We pave the way to success by being prepared, as success is simply the intersection of preparation and opportunity.

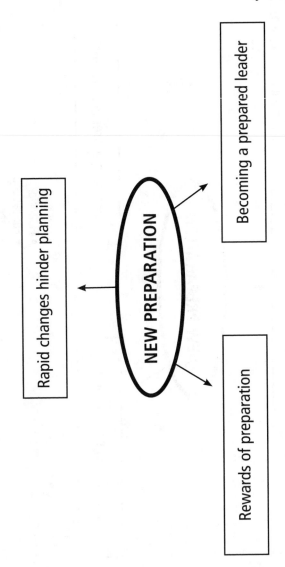

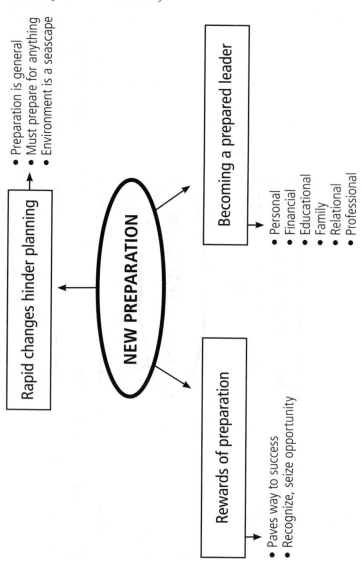

Rapid changes hinder planning
- Preparation is general
- Must prepare for anything
- Environment is a seascape

NEW PREPARATION

Becoming a prepared leader
- Personal
- Financial
- Educational
- Family
- Relational
- Professional

Rewards of preparation
- Paves way to success
- Recognize, seize opportunity

8

NEW POSSIBILITIES

"The future is not the result of choices among
alternative paths offered by the present, but a place
that is created—created first in the mind and will,
created next in activity."[25]
—John H. Schaar

Have you ever considered what makes your destiny so compelling? Do you wonder exactly what it is that draws you onward? Have you ever thought about why the music of your destiny attracts you in the first place? Your destiny is attractive simply because it's a place overflowing with new possibilities. It's a picture of a future that's filled with hope. And it's not just any future; it's *your* future.

Many pages in this book describe the various challenges you'll encounter on your journey to fulfilling your destiny. While all challenges are difficult, they are not the end of our story. The flip side is that each time you respond to a challenge,

---

25. John H. Schaar, *Legitimacy in the Modern State* (New Brunswick, NJ: Transaction Publishers, 1981, 1989), 321.

you open the door to new possibilities in your life and in your organization. As you climb the ladder to your destiny, you will be transformed.

Don't expect it to happen suddenly or even to be noticeable for some time.

IT'S NOT JUST ANY FUTURE; IT'S YOUR FUTURE.

Gradually, you will find that you've abandoned certain characteristics and traits in favor of newer, stronger ones. As a leader transformed by your journey, you'll find yourself empowered to infuse your organization with this new life.

TRAITS OF TRANSFORMED LEADERS

John H. Schaar described the future as "a place that is created—created first in the mind and will, created next in activity." Our destiny, or our future, is certainly a place that we create. And along the way, our journey transforms our attitudes, thinking, and commitments.

In particular, I've found that leaders journeying toward their destinies tend to have:

+ *Altered Attitudes.* The challenges leaders endure can produce a readiness to embrace change, an amazing adaptability to unexpected events, and a heart that's increasingly sensitive to others.

+ *Transformed Thinking.* The situations leaders encounter create in them an intellectual hunger, producing lifelong learners and creative leaders, who are up to date with the latest technologies.

+ *Uncommon Commitments.* Leaders on the journey to their destiny also develop a passion for communicating, and become skilled in engineering organizations for the future.

Altered Attitudes

Leaders possess the trait of change readiness—they are much more inclined to embrace change than to resist it, which can produce vast gains.

Consider how much more you could accomplish by being less controlling and more trusting of others. Think of the freedom that would come with being more aware of your own need of change, as well as the obstacles that might stop you from making necessary changes.

WHEN UNANTICIPATED CIRCUMSTANCES THREATEN, TRANSFORMED LEADERS DON'T BECOME RIGID, DEMANDING, OR CONTROLLING.

Change readiness also makes leaders more of a change advocate within their organization, people who are able to promote change and help others deal with loss. They also help their organization become a leader in change, a powerhouse that moves faster and gets ahead of the pack with a can-do attitude.

THEIR UNCOMMON *SENSITIVITY* MAKES THEM INCLUSIVE.

When unanticipated circumstances threaten, transformed leaders don't become rigid, demanding, or controlling. Their adaptability enables them not to be thrown by the unexpected. Instead, they fluidly travel with the flow of reality, making adjustments and redirecting as necessary to remain on course. Like trapeze artists, they've learned to maneuver courageously and trust their instincts. They never seem to lose their forward momentum.

TRANSFORMED LEADERS BECOME LOVERS AND ADVOCATES OF LIFELONG LEARNING.

Furthermore, transformed leaders don't roll over top of others while moving forward. Their uncommon sensitivity makes them inclusive rather than exclusive. They don't play favorites. They've learned to celebrate cultural differences, as well as to honor the complementary force that God deposited in both genders, capably harnessing this synergy in the workplace.

And this sensitivity extends even to other generations. They look to bridge the generation gap, which is no longer about sex, drugs, and rock and roll but about technology. Transformed leaders understand these issues and actively seek ways to expand their circle to welcome Baby Boomers, Gen Xers, and Millennials.

Transformed Thinking

Transformed leaders are also characterized by transformed thinking. Their curiosity is stimulated by increasingly challenging situations, and they are lovers and advocates of lifelong learning. They read widely, investigate outside of their own disciplines, and probe others with insightful questions. They're inquisitive explorers of the world around them, and are always encouraging others to expand their own borders.

Transformed leaders have internalized Don Herold's statement "It takes a lot of things to prove you are smart but only one thing to prove you are ignorant." They

"IT TAKES A LOT OF THINGS TO PROVE YOU ARE SMART, BUT ONLY ONE THING TO PROVE THAT YOU ARE IGNORANT."

know that the phrase "knowledge is power" is truer today than ever before. They recognize that information is the new currency, and that this intellectual capital multiplies as they barter knowledge. You'll find them willingly sharing what they know. They've realized that innovation—in both speed and quality—is success, so they invest rather than hoard their currency.

They're the type of people who want to invest an hour each day in independent study. Why? Because they've realized that by scheduling time for study, even the average person can develop into an expert in three to five years. They're excited by that possibility.

A VISION WITHOUT A STRATEGY IS ONLY A DREAM. Ask them about their greatest pleasure in life, and they'll talk about their love for accomplishing what others say cannot be done. How? Well, it all starts with their thinking:

+ *Strategic thinking.* Transformed leaders know that a vision without a strategy is only a dream, and that they cannot be strategic if their efforts lack context. They'll praise a systems approach while simultaneously working hard to prevent these efforts from becoming overly complicated. They sagely recognize simplicity as competitive advantage.

+ *Genius thinking.* Despite their busy schedules and massive workloads, leaders can quickly spot networking opportunities and possibilities that others miss. That's what makes them leaders. They pioneer new ways of thinking and demonstrate their genius by seeing through things, as well as seeing things through.

LEADERS RECOGNIZE THAT SIMPLICITY IS A COMPETITIVE ADVANTAGE.

+ *Oblique thinking.* Instead of either-or mentalities, transformed leaders have both-and mentalities. Their thoughts extend beyond vertical and horizontal limits; theirs is more of an angular reality. This orientation illuminates a wealth of possibilities in what others might refer to as impossible.

Transformed leaders are nothing like the executives of one prominent telecommunications firm, who nearly had to be forced to begin using computers. Instead, transformed leaders are characterized by *technophilia*, a willingness to embrace emerging technologies.

LEADERS CAN QUICKLY SPOT RELATIONSHIPS AND POSSIBILITIES THAT OTHERS MISS.

They realize the inherent technical aspects of even the most common organizational activities: how an usher greets you, how funds are raised, how a presentation is collated for an upcoming board meeting. They know that information is power, so they capitalize on information technology to send and receive newsletters, messages, and so forth.

Transformed church leaders can gently remind their critics that the Reformation resulted from the church's use of the printing press. They should not be shy about adopting business technology to improve their effectiveness and efficiency, or to measure results.

TRANSFORMED LEADERS ARE ADEPT AT "FUTURING."

Uncommon Commitments

Transformed leaders are very aware of the need of communication across generations, across cultures, across the small globe that we inhabit, and they are committed to strengthen communication and understanding among them.

They understand how even the most familiar terms can be misunderstood. Some Baby Boomers may interpret the question "Why?" as a disrespectful affront to authority, but transformed leaders recognize a sincere quest for information when they see it.

They firmly believe that cross-cultural communication is not a course of study limited to those who travel or work overseas. They see the world's residents daily in their own churches, organizations, and neighborhoods.

NEW POSSIBILITIES BECOME A NATURAL, EVERYDAY OCCURRENCE.

And, most importantly, transformed leaders are adept at "futuring." They forecast trends by scanning the horizon, clearly envisioning future scenarios. While others are locked in the past or the present, they actively create the future through their decisions and actions.

You'll find them wondering what the world will be like when the current crop of first graders graduate from high school. They intentionally focus portions of their leadership meetings on demographics, on economic and competitive realities that your organization will face five years from now.

And they capably equip their organization to create their own desired future. Like Sherpa guides, they lead others up steep mountains to grasp a vision of the organization's future success. And once they lead their associates into this inspiring future state, they capably direct them in developing and using the skills and perspectives that will transform their vision into a reality.

UNLOCKING A WEALTH OF POSSIBILITIES

Leaders who are willing to think and act this way experience no shortage of new possibilities. In fact, new possibilities become natural, everyday occurrences to them. Theirs is a future of limitless opportunity, boundless growth, and unparalleled resources.

However, focusing on new possibilities doesn't exempt them from experiencing their share of lean times and trying circumstances. Their

ROSE-COLORED GLASSES DO NOT MAGICALLY ENABLE LEADERS TO DECLARE THAT EVERY GLASS IS HALF FULL.

rose-colored glasses do not magically enable them to declare that every glass is half full.

Instead, leaders with broadened and transformed perspectives focus on new possibilities in spite of their circumstances. As they climb the ladder to their God-given destiny, they keep their eyes on the horizon. And at that altitude, they are the first to see the sunrise, the first to perceive the new possibilities that can emerge from any and all situations.

NEW POSSIBILITIES CAN EMERGE FROM ANY AND ALL SITUATIONS.

So you see, leader, new possibilities can become milestone markers that light the road to your destiny. Each new possibility is evidence that you're moving closer to your desired destination!

TEACHING POINTS

1. Leaders who climb the ladder to their destiny are transformed by their journey.

2. They experience altered attitudes, transformed thinking, and uncommon commitments.

3. Altered attitudes

    a. Leaders have a change readiness that allows them to willingly embrace change, producing vast gains.

        i. Leaders are adaptable. They are not thrown off balance by unanticipated circumstances.

        ii. Leaders are sensitive to others, celebrating differences and honoring the complementary skills in both genders. They are inclusive rather than exclusive.

    b. Transformed thinkingLeaders are lifelong learners. They recognize that information is the new currency, and that this intellectual capital multiplies as knowledge is exchanged.

    i. Leaders are creative, accomplishing what others say is impossible by thinking strategically, spotting possibilities that others miss, and embracing both-and mentalities.

    ii. Characterized by technophilia, leaders willingly embrace technology, using it to measure results and improve effectiveness.

  c. Uncommon commitments

    i. Leaders are aware of the need to extend communication to generations, cultures, and around the globe.

    ii. Leaders are adept at "futuring," forecasting trends and future scenarios, and creating the future through today's decisions.

4. Leaders who think and act in these ways experience no shortage of new possibilities.

5. They recognize that new possibilities can emerge from any and all situations.

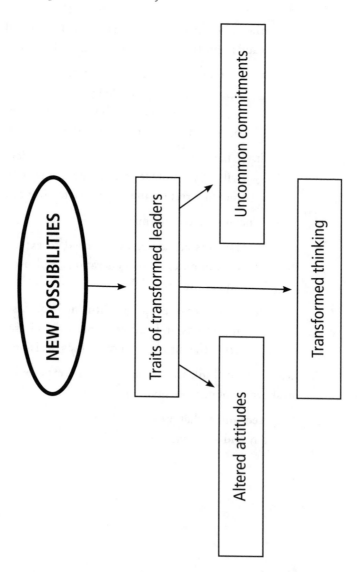

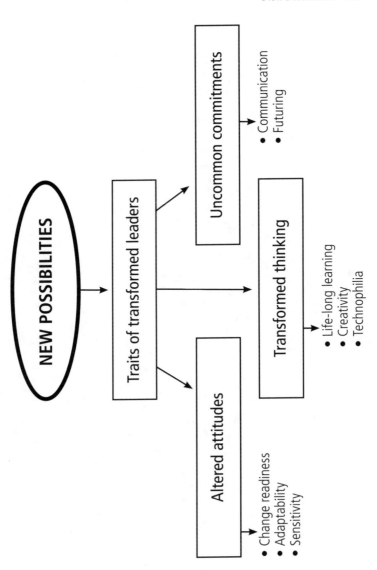

ABOUT THE AUTHOR

In 1973, who would have thought student Sam Chand, who was serving Beulah Heights Bible College as janitor, cook, and dishwasher, would return to the same college in 1989 as President Samuel Chand? Under his leadership, Beulah Heights became the country's largest predominantly African-American Bible college. Today, Dr. Sam Chand is a former pastor, college president, and chancellor, who now serves as president emeritus of Beulah Heights University. In this season of his life, Dr. Sam Chand is focusing on one thing—leadership development. The singular vision of his life is to "Help Others Succeed." Dr. Chand develops leaders through:

- Leadership consultations
- Leadership resources (books, CDs, DVDs)
- Leadership speaking
- Dream Releaser Coaching
- Dream Releaser Publishing

Being raised in a pastor's home in India has uniquely equipped Dr. Sam Chand to share his passion—mentoring, developing, and inspiring leaders to exceed all limits, both in ministry and in the marketplace.

As a Dream Releaser, he serves pastors, ministries, and businesses as a Leadership Architect and Change Strategist. Dr. Chand speaks regularly at leadership conferences, churches, corporations, ministerial conferences, seminars, and other leadership development opportunities.

In addition to this, Dr. Chand...

- Consults with large churches and businesses on leadership and capacity-enhancing issues.
- Was named in the Top-30 Global Leadership Gurus list.
- Is founder and president of Dream Releaser Coaching and Dream Releaser Publishing.
- Conducts nationwide leadership conferences.
- Serves on the board of Beulah Heights University
- Serves on the board of Advisors of EQUIP (Dr. John Maxwell's ministry), which equips five million leaders worldwide.

Leaders around the world are using Dr. Chand's writings as textbooks in leadership development. His books include *8 Steps to Achieve Your Destiny, Leadership Pain, Cracking Your Church's Culture Code, Futuring, Who's Holding Your Ladder?, What's Shaking Your Ladder?, Who Moved Your Ladder?,*

Ladder Focus, *Planning Your Succession*, *Failure: The Womb of Success*, and *Weathering the Storm*.

Dr. Chand holds an honorary Doctor of Humane Letters from Beulah Heights University, an honorary Doctor of Divinity from Heritage Bible College, a Master of Arts in Biblical Counseling from Grace Theological Seminary, and a Bachelor of Arts in Biblical Education from Beulah Heights University.

Dr. Chand shares his life and love with his wife, Brenda, daughters Rachel and Deborah, son-in-law, Zack, and grand-daughters Adeline and Rose.

For more information, please contact:

Samuel R. Chand Consulting, Inc.

950 Eagles Landing Parkway, Suite 295

Stockbridge, GA 30281 USA

www.samchand.com